CULTURES OF THE WORLD

Estonia

Cavendish Square
New York

ESTONIA TODAY

ESTONIA IS A SINGING NATION. MUSIC PLAYS A VITAL ROLE in the culture, life, and politics of Estonia, a small, northern country of 1.3 million people located on the Baltic Sea. Estonians think of themselves as a people who sang their way to freedom.

For most of recorded history, Estonia was occupied by a succession of foreign powers: the Swedes, the Russians, and the Germans. All left their distinct traces on Estonian cultural life. However, regardless of which of their neighbors was occupying their land, for eight hundred years the Estonian people stayed in the same powerless position. Estonians were serfs, tied to the land, forced to obey powerful foreign landlords who could control every aspect of their lives, including where they lived and who they married.

In the nineteenth century, when Russia controlled Estonia, Estonian men were subject to military conscription by lottery. In 1841, the British writer Lady Elizabeth Eastlake wrote movingly of the Estonian people's bleak situation:

> From the moment that the peasant of the Baltic provinces draws the fatal lot no. 1, he knows that he is ... a Russian soldier, and not only himself, but every son from that hour born to him; for, like the executioner's office in Germany, a soldier's life

is hereditary ... If wars and climate and sickness and hardship spare him, he returns after four-and-twenty years of service—his language scarce remembered, his religion changed, and with not a ruble in his pocket—to seek his daily bread by his own exertions for the remainder of his life, or to be chargeable to his parish, who by this time have forgotten that he ever existed, and certainly wish he had never returned.

Despite this oppression, the nineteenth century saw a flowering of distinctively Estonian arts, music, and culture. It was during this period, known as the "awakening," that the seeds were planted for Estonian independence.

Following the collapse of czarist Russia in 1917, Estonians gained home rule and, ultimately, independence. But this independence was short-lived due to Estonia's small size and vulnerable geographic position. Estonia, like its Baltic neighbors Latvia and Lithuania, is squeezed between Germany and Russia, which have long been larger and more powerful nations. Located between two larger powers, Estonia was treated as a bargaining chip. In 1939, Nazi Germany made a pact with Soviet Russia: Germany would allow Russia to occupy Estonia if Russia would not retaliate when Germany occupied Poland. That was how, after just twenty years, Estonia lost its independence—but it had not lost its voice.

Even though the Soviets forbade Estonians to express patriotic sentiments about an independent Estonia, the Estonians continued to voice their patriotism in song. By singing, they carried Estonian cultural heritage into the twenty-first century, and they kept the flame of independence alive. In the late 1980s, when the Soviet Union was weakening, a popular social movement rose up in Estonia. The Singing Revolution started as a sing-along. Attendees at one of Estonia's many music festivals began spontaneously singing patriotic, pro-Estonian music, much of it coming from the nineteenth-century period of awakening. Over the next three years, these sing-alongs grew in size and number and culminated in a multinational sing-along. Two million people across Estonia and the other occupied Baltic states (Latvia and Lithuania) joined hands and sang patriotic national songs to demand their independence. In 1991, when the Estonian Congress declared independence, Soviet tanks arrived to destroy radio towers and television stations and thereby stop the spread of news. Masses of singing protesters put their bodies between the tanks and the radio towers and TV stations, forcing the Soviets to retreat. It was through this Singing Revolution that Estonians gained their freedom.

In the nearly thirty years since their 1991 independence, Estonia has continued its musical traditions; every five years, the Estonian Song Celebration hosts the world's largest choir (in 2014, over thirty thousand singers, from all parts of Estonia, participated). At the same time, Estonia has transitioned into a successful parliamentary democracy and joined the European Union. Estonians have chosen leaders who promote free-market ideas and embrace technology as key to a successful twenty-first-century economy. In 1991, only half of Estonia's residents even had telephone lines. By the year 2000, nearly all of Estonia's schools had internet access. Government-provided free Wi-Fi access is available across the nation. Currently, computer programming is part of the school curriculum along with reading and writing; students begin learning coding in first grade.

Estonia is a Baltic nation that shares a border with Latvia to the south and Russia to the east.

Estonia, long a small, isolated country subject to its powerful neighbors, liberated itself through song. It is now asserting itself as a global leader in an increasingly post-national, high-tech world. Some Estonians worry that the nation's increasingly global mindset will alter the distinctive musical and cultural traditions that have long been a powerful force in Estonian life. Still, the summer music festivals continue to draw large crowds. Today, Estonians from all generations see the summer music festivals as opportunities to promote national unity and celebrate their independent nation.

GEOGRAPHY

To the north of Estonia is the Gulf of Finland;
to the west is the Baltic Sea. Estonia shares
its southern border with Latvia.

THE REPUBLIC OF ESTONIA (EESTI Vabariik in Estonian) is washed by the cold waters of the Gulf of Finland to the north and the Baltic Sea to the west. It shares a border with Latvia to the south. Lake Peipsi (also known as Lake Peipus) and the Narva River form part of the border between Estonia and its eastern neighbor, Russia. This small former Soviet republic is 17,463 square miles (45,228 square kilometers) in area—about half the size of Maine, but with the same population.

Much of Estonia borders the sea; including the islands, Estonia has 2,357 miles (3,794 kilometers) of highly indented coastline. The rural western coast and Estonia's Baltic Sea islands, characterized by beaches, parks, and wildlife, are sources of both national pride and tourism in Estonia. While Latvia and Russia are Estonia's nearest neighbors overland, culturally Estonia has a closer affinity with Scandinavia. Helsinki is a short ferry ride across the Gulf of Finland from Estonia's capital, Tallinn, and Estonian and Finnish are linguistic cousins. Finns and Estonians can understand each other without much difficulty.

Geographically, the coastal regions in Estonia's north and west are low-lying and marshy. Inland, where elevation averages 161 feet (49 meters) above sea level, much of the country is a flat, forested plain.

HISTORY

Estonians cheer for their country.

ESTONIANS HAVE BEEN AN ETHNIC group for thousands of years, but they have rarely had the opportunity to form a self-determining nation. Their traditional lands have always been surrounded by more powerful neighbors. With Germany and Poland to the west, Russia to the east, and Sweden across the Baltic Sea, Estonia was passed back and forth among these dominant powers for nearly a thousand years. As a result, Estonian architecture and culture bears the markings of Scandinavian, Russian, Polish, and German influence.

It wasn't until 1918 that Estonia became an independent nation—and that only lasted for two decades. In 1939, Estonia's neighbors, Germany and Russia, used Estonia as a bargaining chip. The two larger countries signed a treaty agreeing that Germany would permit Russia to annex the Baltic states (Estonia, Latvia, Lithuania) as well as parts of Finland, if Russia wouldn't intervene when Germany invaded Poland. Estonia would continue to belong to the Soviet Union until its collapse in 1991, when Estonia became an independent nation—for the second time. The painful, defiant, and proud history of Estonia is expressed eloquently in

In 1988, US president Ronald Reagan declared his support for Estonian independence, saying: "Our government has never recognized the forcible incorporation of the Baltic States into the Soviet Union, and we never will. The American people, citizens of a land conceived in liberty and dedicated to equality under God for all, support the aspirations of the Baltic people to regain the freedom that was theirs and to chart their own course."

SOVIET RULE

War casualties, deportations, and fleeing refugees reduced Estonia's population from a prewar level of 1.13 million to 850,000 by the end of the 1940s. An anti-Russian resistance continued to fight from forest bases but was unsuccessful against the might of the Soviet army.

During Soviet rule, many Estonians were deported by train to the USSR.

The 1950s were a difficult time for Estonians, and many people suffered under Soviet dictator Joseph Stalin's harsh regime. Political opponents, intellectuals, and anyone believed to be a German collaborator were deported to Siberian labor camps. The total number deported was around 60,000. The Soviet administration also introduced cultural Russification in a systematic attempt to eradicate Estonian national consciousness. Estonian history was rewritten, national monuments destroyed, and books suppressed.

Despite Soviet oppression, Estonian national consciousness remained strong. In the post-Stalin era, Estonians began to demonstrate for civil rights. Dissent in the Baltic states reached its height in 1979, on the fortieth anniversary of the Molotov-Ribbentrop Pact.

WINNING INDEPENDENCE (YET AGAIN)

Soviet president Mikhail Gorbachev's policies of glasnost, or openness, and perestroika, or restructuring, led to greater political freedom in Estonia. Estonian cultural life flourished, a free press developed, political parties were formed, and religion was openly practiced again. The "awakening" began with massive environmental demonstrations protesting Moscow's plans for strip-mining in northern Estonia. In 1989, the Communist government of Estonia declared its "sovereignty," a move rejected by Gorbachev. After the first-ever free Soviet elections in 1990, the new government of Estonia declared independence on March 30, 1990.

In August 1991, a failed military coup in Moscow by Communist hard-liners effectively ousted Gorbachev and led to the breakup of the Soviet

Union. Estonia declared full independence on August 20, 1991. It declined to join the successor to the USSR, the Commonwealth of Independent States (CIS), preferring to sever ties with Russia.

Since independence, Estonia has embraced a multiparty parliamentary-style democracy that has relied heavily on coalitions to form governments. Despite a number of parliamentary scandals, Estonian democracy has thrived as the economy has grown from strength to strength. Estonia has become more integrated with the culture and economy of Western Europe, with the government achieving its long-term aim of joining the European Union in 2004, as well as joining the North Atlantic Treaty Organization (NATO) the same year. Estonia adopted the euro as official currency in 2011 and has pioneered a new model of citizenship for the digital era. Estonia is a founding member of the D5 (Digital 5), now Digital 7, a group of governments including Israel, Canada, Uruguay, New Zealand, and South Korea who work together to strengthen the global digital economy. The Estonian government now offers "e-residency" for global digital citizens, enabling individuals located anywhere in the world to register with the Estonian government and virtually run a business in Estonia.

Estonians celebrate their restored independence.

INTERNET LINKS

http://www.einst.ee/en
This is the official website for the Estonian Institute, which spreads information about Estonian society and culture abroad.

http://www.estonica.org/en/history
This online encyclopedia about Estonia offers information about history, society, and culture.

http://www.hoeckmann.de/germany/baltics.htm
This site offers historical maps of Germany and the Baltics.

GOVERNMENT

The Estonian Riigikogu (parliament) is housed in Tallinn.

ESTONIA HAS SUCCEEDED IN THE remarkable challenge of building and sustaining an independent, democratic system of government after the collapse of the Soviet Union in 1991. Estonia uses a multiparty, parliamentary system of government, where voters elect representatives in the legislative assembly (the Riigikogu). The leader of the party that wins the most seats in the Riigikogu typically becomes the prime minister and head of government. The members of the Riigikogu vote to elect the president. The president is head of state.

The multiparty, parliamentary system ensures that power is shared among competing factions. For a prime minister to succeed—and keep his or her party in power—he or she must build a coalition with opposing parties to maintain majority support in the Riigikogu. For example, as of 2018, Prime Minister Jüri Ratas, leader of the Center Party, heads a coalition government supported by both the leftist Social Democrats (SDE) and the Union of Pro Patria and Res Publica (IRL), a conservative party. While Estonia has six major political parties, the government

In 2015, Defense Minister Sven Mikser had to leave his post due to a reorganization in the government. He cracked a joke, tweeting: "How do you know when you're not a minister anymore? It's when you get into the back seat of your car—and it doesn't go anywhere."

Kersti Kaljulaid, Estonia's first woman president, brings a tech-savvy, forward-thinking approach to governance. She is included in Forbes' *list of the world's one hundred most powerful women and is quoted as saying, "I represent the only truly digital society which actually has a state; almost all our citizens' interactions with the government, including voting, can be done securely online, and our 'e-residents' can incorporate and run their businesses in Estonia without ever having to set foot here." It's not yet known how the traditional model of the nation-state will be transformed by globalization and the digital revolution of the twenty-first century, but it is clear that Estonia's president is anticipating any changes in governance the digital era may require.*

has consistently supported free-market reforms intended to grow Estonia's economy, which is now one of the most robust in the former Soviet Union.

Some of Estonia's political divisions reflect differing attitudes toward non-Estonians, including foreigners, asylum-seekers, and refugees. Former president Toomas Hendrik Ilves reflected in 2016 that Syrian refugees are not terrorists and advocated for acceptance of all who wish, like the Estonian people, to live in freedom. He contrasted his tolerant attitude with perspectives from the far right, saying, "US soldiers are in Estonia to protect us, and if necessary, to fight for our freedom. For this, they deserve respect, at the very least. Not the recommendation made by a local politician ... that Afro-American soldiers should wear their uniforms at all times in order to avoid confrontations."

Former president Lennart Meri attributes Estonia's success to its flexibility, as a small nation, to change directions. "Compared to Russia," Meri has stated, "Estonia is like an Inuit kayak. A supertanker takes 16 nautical miles to turn around, but the Inuit can do a 180 degree turn on a dime." In 2016, Estonia's parliament made a change of direction by electing the nation's first woman president, Kersti Kaljulaid.

POSTINDEPENDENCE POLITICS

With a great many parties contesting elections since independence, coalition government has become the norm in Estonian politics. In the nearly three decades since independence, Estonia has seen ten prime ministers. Estonia's current political system dates from 1992, when a new constitution was adopted following a referendum, which provided for a 101-seat parliament, the Riigikogu, and a presidency with limited powers. Estonia's first free parliamentary elections were held in September of the same year, with thirty-eight parties participating. The conservative Fatherland alliance won twenty-nine seats, making it the largest party in the Riigikogu. The leader of the Fatherland alliance, Mart Laar, became prime minister of a coalition government.

Jüri Ratas, prime minister of Estonia and leader of the Center Party

The new center-right government possessed few links with the old Soviet establishment. Several ministers were younger than thirty-five years old, while many others were recently returned émigrés, or refugees. Following a series of scandals and political defections, Laar was forced to resign as prime minister in 1994. He was replaced by Andres Tarand, leader of the moderates.

Estonia's second postindependence parliamentary election, held in 1995, was contested by thirty parties. Forty-one seats were won by an alliance of the Estonian Coalition Party and the Rural Union. A coalition of the newly established Estonian Reform Party won nineteen seats, and the Estonian Center Party gained sixteen seats. For the first time, the Russian minority was represented in the Riigikogu, by the Our Home Is Estonia alliance, which won six seats. Tiit Vähi, leader of the Estonian Coalition Party, became prime minister. Vähi resigned as prime minister on February 25, 1997, following allegations of corrupt real estate dealings in Tallinn. The deputy chairman of the Estonian Coalition Party, Mart Siimann, a former journalist, was nominated the new prime minister.

In parliamentary elections in 1999, the People's Party Moderates formed a coalition with Mart Laar as prime minister. In January 2002, Laar stepped down again, and Siim Kallas was appointed prime minister, leading a coalition of the

Presents since
independence:
Lennart Meri,
1992-2001;
Arnold Rüütel,
2001-2006;
Toomas Hendrik
Ilves, 2006-2016;
Kersti Kaljulaid,
2016-present.

Reform Party and the Center Party. Juhan Parts led a coalition of the Res Publica Party, the Estonian Reform Party, and the People's Union to form a government following the parliamentary election in 2003. Parts resigned in 2005 following a no-confidence vote in the Riigikogu against one of his ministers, and the president nominated Estonian Reform Party leader Andrus Ansip as prime minister. Ansip formed a new government, the eighth in twelve years. Ansip served as prime minister until 2014, when he resigned. Taavi Rõivas (at that time just thirty-four, and the youngest head of a European government), also of the Reform Party, became prime minister. In November 2016, the parliament voted that they had no confidence in Rõivas's administration. A new coalition government was formed, led by Jüri Ratas, who became prime minister on November 23, 2016. Ratas advocates for a national emphasis on technology because "falling behind is not an option. The world will not wait for us."

THE PRESIDENCY

The president of the republic is the head of state. The president is elected for a term of five years by a secret ballot in the Riigikogu and must gain a two-thirds majority. Presidential candidates must be Estonian citizens and at least forty years old. The president's duties are mainly ceremonial, including representing Estonia in international relations and carrying out various diplomatic duties. The president is also responsible for initiating amendments to the constitution, declaring elections for the Riigikogu, and nominating candidates for the post of prime minister.

Estonia's first presidential elections, held in fall 1992, were inconclusive; no candidate won a majority, but four main candidates emerged. Following a second round of voting, Lennart Meri was declared the winner. Meri, an intellectual famous for his films and writings on Estonian history and culture, held the position until 2001. In 2001, Arnold Rüütel was elected president, holding the position for one term. In 2006, Toomas Hendrik Ilves became president. An experienced politician, Ilves was the leader of the Social Democratic Party in the 1990s, and he later became a member of the European Parliament. Ilves held the office until 2016; since the Estonian presidency is term-limited, Ilves retired from politics at that time. Kersti Kaljulaid became president in 2016.

THE LEGISLATURE

Legislative power rests with Estonia's state assembly, the Riigikogu. The Riigikogu's 101 members are elected for a term of four years by a system of proportional representation. They must be twenty-one years or older. Estonian citizens over the age of eighteen can vote in national elections and referendums. The Riigikogu adopts laws, decides on the holding of referendums, elects the president of the republic, and ratifies the national budget. The Riigikogu also elects from its members a chairman who directs the work and procedures of the assembly.

Jüri Ratas stands with members of his cabinet in 2016.

Executive power is held by the Council of Ministers, which is formed from members of the Riigikogu. The Council of Ministers consists of the prime minister, who is the head of the government, and other ministers. The prime minister has the task of forming the Council of Ministers, whose members are usually selected from the leading political parties. The Council of Ministers implements policy decisions and legislation, coordinates the work of government institutions, submits draft legislation to the Riigikogu, and organizes relations with foreign states.

PARTY POLITICS

Eleven parties ran in the most recent election, in 2015, and six of these gained seats in the Riigikogu: the Estonian Reform Party and the Estonian Center Party (which are both liberal parties, the latter being very popular among Russian voters), the conservative Estonian Conservative People's Party and Union of Pro Patria and Res Publica Party, the leftist Social Democratic Party, and the center-right Free Party.

For a party to be legally registered, it must have at least one thousand members. In elections, a party must gain at least 5 percent of the vote to be awarded a seat in the Riigikogu. Most of the larger political parties campaign on the basis of a complete economic and social program, while smaller parties, such as the ethnic Russian Party in Estonia, represent the interests of a particular group or campaign on a single issue.

At the World Congress of Finno-Ugric Peoples in 2008, Estonian president Toomas Hendrik Ilves met Russian president Dmitry Medvedev, marking the first official meeting between presidents of the two countries since the collapse of the Soviet Union.

LOCAL POLITICS

Under Soviet administration, there were no local governing bodies. Following independence, Estonia introduced a system of local government, which divided the nation into local legislative bodies. This system was reformed in 2017, with some legislative districts merging with one another, reducing the number of districts and increasing the number of voters per district.

Currently, local governing bodies are split into fifteen cities and sixty-four municipalities. According to Jaak Aab, minister of public administration, "Where prior to the mergers we had 169 municipalities with fewer than 5,000 residents, now there are only 15. In addition, the average number of residents per municipality has grown threefold. These figures alone demonstrate that our municipalities are now more capable and able to perform all of the duties that we assigned to them with extra money, including those of county governments."

The local government carries out administrative functions, manages state property, and provides services. The increase of local government responsibilities has been severely hampered by a lack of finances. Local government is funded by the national government. All Estonian citizens can vote in local elections, as can residents who are not citizens. In 2015, the voting age was lowered to sixteen for all local elections. As Andres Anvelt, then the minister of justice, explained, "Studies indicate that after finishing basic school, kids are aware of the political scenery and are taking active steps to participate in politics, for example establishing youth councils or organizing shadow elections. Therefore, I find it reasonable that 16-year-olds have the right to vote at local elections."

JUSTICE SYSTEM

Justice is administered solely by Estonia's courts. Rural and city courts hear cases at the local level. District courts can review the decisions of the lower courts, and the Supreme Court, the highest court in the land, is the ultimate court of appeal. The chief judge is appointed by the president, with the approval of parliament, and serves a nine-year term. The chief justice then selects the other justices on the Supreme Court and they remain judges for life.

As in most other democracies, all defendants in Estonia are assumed innocent until proven guilty, and all defendants have the right to legal representation in court. The constitution provides that all court proceedings be held in public. Suspects can be held for forty-eight hours without being formally charged, while further detention requires a court order. Suspects can be arrested only with a warrant issued by a court. Estonia's police force was formed in 1991 from the remnants of the Soviet militia and comes under the Ministry of Internal Affairs.

MILITARY

Following the breakup of the Soviet Union, Estonia did not have an army. Russia maintained military bases in Estonia until 1994. In April 1992, Estonia established its own Ministry of Defense and an independent military, with the military firmly under civilian control. According to the constitution, the president is the supreme commander of the armed forces. The Estonian Regular Armed Forces employs about six thousand troops. Estonia has compulsory military service for young men; about half of the Regular Armed Forces is comprised of conscripts.

Since the mid-1990s, Estonia has sent troops on peacekeeping missions, in particular to Afghanistan and Kosovo. Estonia has also supported the United States in overseas military operations and contributed a force to the occupation of Iraq in 2005, although all Estonian troops were withdrawn in 2009 to be redeployed to Afghanistan, where Estonian peacekeeping forces continue to be stationed. Estonia joined NATO in March 2004. Most Estonians support their country's membership in NATO, since it offers them protection against more powerful neighbors.

After Russia annexed Crimea in 2014, Estonians became increasingly wary of their powerful neighbor. Estonia's membership in NATO ensures wider support from other military forces in Europe and beyond, but Estonians began to doubt NATO's support after the United States elected Donald Trump as president in 2016. Trump has threatened to withdraw from NATO and is viewed by many as sympathetic to Russian interests. As a result of these changes in the geopolitical order, Estonians have swelled the ranks of the Estonian Defense

Estonia was one of the first nations to experience the destructive, yet bloodless, results of a cyberattack. On April 27, 2007, cyber attackers managed to shut down government, banking, and communication services by spamming servers. They used automated bots to overwhelm websites with traffic, causing them to crash. The attacks impacted many segments of Estonian society. Citizens found themselves unable to use ATMs. Government workers couldn't send email. Journalists couldn't receive or broadcast news. This situation took weeks to resolve and left Estonians determined to be prepared for future cyberattacks.

According to state cyber-defense expert Liisa Past, "Cyber aggression is very different to kinetic warfare." She explains, "It allows you to create confusion, while staying well below the level of an armed attack." One reason that cyberattacks can be so destructive is that treaty agreements did not anticipate the emergence of cyberwarfare. For example, Estonia is a member of NATO, and the NATO treaty agreement specifies that member countries provide military aid to any member nation that is attacked. But since the cyberattack created no direct physical damage, NATO members were not obligated to offer military support to Estonia.

Cyber warfare poses an additional defensive challenge: attacks may or may not come from a nation state. It can be difficult to tell whether a cyberattack originates with a government or whether hackers, copycats, or opportunists have taken advantage of a diplomatic crisis to attack. While many say that the Russian government initiated the Estonian cyberattacks, there is still no definitive proof.

broadcasters, were swamped and virtually disabled by a series of massive cyberattacks. Some observers were of the opinion that the attacks originated from Russian hackers. The attacks had important implications for Estonia's defense network and banking systems. Since that time, the Estonian Defense League has created a volunteer army of cybersecurity experts, who donate their time and expertise to create contingency plans in case of cyberattacks.

Following Russia's annexation of Crimea in 2014, Estonia, Finland, and other Baltic states have become concerned about Russia's territorial ambitions. While the NATO alliance guarantees military to support to Estonia in case of invasion, Estonians hesitate to trust this commitment, especially since the election of Donald Trump to the United States presidency. Trump threatened to withdraw from NATO, or threatened to levy defense fees from NATO members, on more than one occasion.

Estonia's relations with its Baltic and Scandinavian neighbors have been far more positive and productive. Since independence, Estonia has sought to re-create its traditional and historical ties with the Nordic countries, especially Finland and Sweden. The Baltic Assembly (BA) was established in 1991 as a forum for the governments of Estonia, Latvia, and Lithuania to discuss common economic, political, and cultural issues. The BA is made up of sixty members—twenty from each country. In 1994, another body, the Baltic Council of Ministers, was set up to allow for direct minister-to-minister contact between the governments of the Baltic countries.

Estonia's trade and cultural ties with Sweden, Finland, and Germany continue to grow. In 2005, Estonia joined the European Union's Nordic Battlegroup. The Estonian government has also shown continued interest in joining the Nordic Council. In 1992, more than 90 percent of Estonia's international trade was with Russia, whereas today three-quarters of foreign investment in Estonia comes from Finland and Sweden, to which Estonia sends more than 31 percent of its exports.

INTERNET LINKS

http://www.bbc.com/news/world-europe-17220810
The BBC's profile of Estonia can be found here. The BBC is also a reliable source for international news.

http://www.estonica.org/en/Society/Development_of_the_Estonian_political_landscape_until_2006
This section of the online Estonian encyclopedia covers various aspects of the country's political landscape.

https://en.portal.santandertrade.com/analyse-markets/estonia/political-outline
Founded by Santander, a well-known global bank, this site offers economic and political information about Estonia and other countries around the world.

ECONOMY

Become an e-Estonian
Join the Digital Society
e-estonia.com/e-residents

Anyone in the world can apply online to
become an e-resident of Estonia.

4

ESTONIA SAW TREMENDOUS economic growth following independence in 1991. It quickly cast off communist approaches in favor of a free-market approach emphasizing economic integration with the EU, support for digital technology, and globalization. Estonia is now rated a high-income country by the World Bank, with a gross domestic product (GDP) per capita that is just $10,000 less than the EU average.

The Estonian government has taken innovative measures to become an easy place to start or run a business. Over a million business owners from all over the world have registered with the Estonian government to become "e-residents" able to digitally conduct their business affairs in Estonia. Estonia's status as an EU member allows e-residents to feel confident of the security and transparency of financial and governmental processes.

In 2014, US president Barack Obama praised Estonia's economic progress, saying: "Estonia is one of the great success stories among the nations that reclaimed their independence after the Cold War. You've built a vibrant democracy and new prosperity, and you've become a model for how citizens can interact with their government in the twenty-first century, something President Ilves has championed."

The Skype technology that allows so many people to speak to each other for free using a microphone and an internet connection was developed in Estonia in 2003. The business was later acquired by eBay, and then by Microsoft.

WHO ARE ESTONIA'S E-RESIDENTS?

An impressive list of global leaders and international luminaries have become e-residents of Estonia. Estonia's celebrity e-residents include: Shinzo Abe, the prime minister of Japan; Angela Merkel, the chancellor of Germany; comedian Trevor Noah (right), host of American comedy series The Daily Show; *and Britain's Prince Andrew, the Duke of York.*

GROWING A CAPITALIST ECONOMY

Historically, Estonia had an agricultural economy. Industrial development in the 1930s changed this, as did the forced collectivization of farms and further industrialization under the Soviets in the 1940s and 1950s. All property and industry were nationalized under Soviet rule. For fifty years Estonia's economy was centrally controlled and directed from Moscow as an integral part of the Soviet Union. Decisions concerning the country's economic and industrial development were made within the context of the whole USSR, and Estonia was subservient to Moscow's broader plans for the USSR as a whole.

Estonia's transformation from a centrally controlled, Soviet-style economy to a free-market economy was miraculously fast. Estonia began the transition to a market economy in the late 1980s with the establishment of a central bank and a private banking system. By mid-1994, only three years after independence, the private sector was generating more than 50 percent of Estonia's GDP. This transformation has not occurred without some suffering for the Estonian people. The winter of 1991—1992 was probably the hardest Estonians have experienced since World War II, with the cost of living increasing tenfold by the end of 1992. This was particularly hard for the people to bear, as Estonia had been one of the wealthiest regions in the USSR before independence.

This collectivized fish farm in Estonia processed and smoked fish during the 1970s.

TRADE AND ECONOMY

Estonia has a well-educated, technically skilled workforce and lower wage rates compared with many of its competitors in Western Europe, making the country very attractive to foreign investors. Companies from Europe and the United States have invested extensively in its timber, textile, and manufacturing industries. Estonia's neighbors Sweden and Finland have been two of its biggest investors and have purchased many of Estonia's newly privatized companies. Major American and Finnish corporations have also invested in the computer, electronics, and automobile industries.

During the past twenty years, the Estonian economy has enjoyed an export-led boom, especially in machinery and equipment, wood and paper, textiles, furniture, metals, and chemical products. Estonia exports goods chiefly to Sweden (18 percent), Finland (16 percent), Latvia (9 percent), Russia (6.5 percent), and Germany (6 percent).

Estonia's main sources of imported goods are Finland (13 percent), Germany (11 percent), Lithuania (9.5 percent), Latvia (8 percent), Sweden (8 percent), Poland (7 percent), the Netherlands (6 percent), Russia (5.5 percent), and China (4 percent). At one time, 70 percent of Estonia's trade was with the Russian Federation, but this has fallen dramatically, in large part because of Estonia's membership in the EU.

In 1994, Estonia became one of the first countries in the world to adopt a flat tax rate, where all workers, regardless of income, pay the same percentage of tax.

GROWTH AND INEQUALITY

Estonia's economy grew very quickly following independence; the rate of growth in the year 2000 was an extraordinary 10 percent. Growth slowed following the global financial crisis in 2008, but the economy recovered relatively quickly. By 2017, Estonia's rate of economic growth was considered "exceptionally high" by the European Commission, and the outlook for future growth was positive. Per-capita incomes have tripled since the year 2000, but it is worth noting that while Estonia's economy has expanded, so, too, has economic inequality within the country. In 1990, the poorest 20 percent of Estonia's citizens owned 10 percent of its wealth; the latest data from the World Bank indicates that the poorest 20 percent of Estonians own just 7 percent of the country's wealth. As of 2015, 21 percent of Estonians lived under the national poverty line.

BANKING AND FINANCE

In recent years Tallinn has emerged as a financial center, with a number of local and international banks having offices there. Estonia was the first former Soviet republic to introduce its own currency, the kroon (meaning "crown"), in June 1992. Estonia adopted the euro as its official currency in 2011.

The average annual income in Estonia in 2016 was $29,040.

FARMING AND FISHING

Combined with fishing, agriculture constitutes only about 3 percent of the country's economic output, down from 10 percent in 1997 and in marked contrast to Estonia's traditional role as an agrarian economy.

For centuries, Estonians referred to themselves as *maarahvas* (MAH-rahh-vus), meaning "people of the land," and the farming lifestyle became a part of the Estonian identity. In the 1930s, the heyday of Estonian agriculture, it was popularly thought that Estonian eggs, butter, and meat graced the breakfast tables of Saint Petersburg and London.

An Estonian dairy worker makes cheese.

In the Soviet era, Estonia's farms were forcibly collectivized and brought under government control. All traditional family farms were nationalized, and many farmers and their families were deported to Siberia. By 1949, Estonia's 140,000 farms had been converted into 2,400 state-run units. In the 1990s the process was reversed, with farms being privatized, reorganized, and reinstated to their former family-run status. Inefficiency remains a problem for Estonia's farms, and farmers have difficulty financing the purchase of modern farming equipment. Consequently, overall agricultural production steadily declined through the 1990s, and many farmers struggle to do more than break even.

Barley, other grains, potatoes, and other vegetables are the principal crops grown. Dairy farms are numerous, and meat, milk, eggs, and butter are the country's chief agricultural products. Estonia's food processing industry meets domestic demand and accounts for 9 percent of exports.

FOREST MANAGEMENT

Estonia's forests, which cover 50 percent of the country, are an obvious natural resource. The exploitation of these forests provides timber for furniture manufacturing, pulp factories, paper goods, and fuel.

Estonians' timber skills and low wage levels have made the country's timber industry highly competitive and successful, with wood and paper products making up 14 percent of exports.

TECH INDUSTRY

Estonia's engineering and electronics industry has grown rapidly since independence, fueled by extensive foreign investment. In 2007, fifteen thousand skilled technicians were employed in the electronics sector by approximately 370 companies. Output has grown fifteenfold, with the electronics industry taking in 238 million euros in 2001, rising to 719 million euros by 2006. In 2006, the electronics industry contributed 11 percent of total industrial output. Products include electronic motors, integrated circuits, cables, and other high-tech products. Factories formerly working for the Soviet military have been successfully adapted to sell to Western markets.

In the past decade, Tallinn has become a hub for technological innovation. Entrepreneur Siim Saare explains that "the numerous incubators, accelerators, and co-working spaces" have helped Tallinn become a nexus of tech start-ups.

TEXTILE INDUSTRY

Estonia's thriving textile industry has adjusted quickly to the demands of a market economy. Estonia exports clothing and footwear products to the rest of Europe and the United States. Furniture and bedding account for 11 percent of Estonia's exports.

MINING AND CHEMICALS

Mineral resources include oil shale, peat, and industrial minerals such as clays, limestone, sand, and gravel. Mineral fuels account for 6 percent of Estonia's exports. Due to oil shale reserves, Estonia is almost entirely energy independent. Estonia has large phosphorite deposits, which are the basis of the fertilizer manufacturing industry. The chemical industry, which contributes more than 4 percent of Estonia's industrial output, produces household chemical products, fertilizers, plastics, paints, and lacquer products.

Oil-shale production is a major driver of Estonia's economy, but it also creates pollution.

ENERGY AND POLLUTION

In the past, Estonia was heavily dependent on Soviet energy supplies. Since independence, the oil-shale industry, centered around Kohtla-Järve, Kiviõli, and Narva, has become Estonia's main source of domestic and industrial energy, making the country virtually independent in electricity production and providing 14 percent of its industrial output. Estonia has abundant supplies of oil shale, estimated at 16.5 billion tons (15 billion metric tons). Most of the oil shale is used to supply thermal power plants, which in turn generate electricity, some of which is then exported to Latvia, the Netherlands, Finland, and Denmark. Estonia also imports small amounts of natural gas from Russia.

Peat and firewood are significant energy sources as well, as are two hydroelectric plants on the Narva River. The government is actively seeking ways to upgrade the thermal power plants to control pollution and limit damage to the environment.

Some Estonian energy experts are calling for Estonia to stop relying on oil shale and to focus instead on renewable energy alternatives. Valdur Lahtvee, founder of the Estonian Green Party and former director of the Stockholm Environment Institute-Tallinn Center, has observed that the "oil shale industry contributes approximately 4 percent of Estonia's GDP, but, at the same time, when you look at total national emissions [oil shale] provides 90 percent of the hazardous waste, about 80 percent of the major air emissions and 70/80 percent of the water used. So, it has a really huge impact to the environment."

TOURISM

Estonia's service industry is the best developed in the former Soviet Union and is one of the country's biggest growth industries. It has developed rapidly since independence and today accounts for almost 69 percent of total GDP. Tourism has been growing steadily since 1990. Foreigners and local residents visit the historic towns of Tallinn and Tartu and experience the tranquility of the rural interior and the coastal resorts and islands of Hiiumaa and Saaremaa.

It is estimated that 2.5 million foreigners visited Estonia in 2008, and 6 million foreigners visited in 2017. Domestic tourists accounted for more than a million visits, with tourism producing nearly 15 percent of Estonia's GDP. The vast majority of international visitors were from neighboring Finland, though significant numbers came from Latvia, Russia, Germany, and Sweden. Ferries have been crossing the Gulf of Finland since 1936, and many Finns take day trips from Helsinki to Tallinn to shop for cheaper goods and see the sights of the Estonian capital. Since independence, there has been a rapid increase in hotels, bed-and-breakfasts, and home stays organized by Western travel agents.

ROADS AND TRANSIT

Estonia gets a lot of business from traffic between Western Europe and Russia. Estonia has good road and rail links with Russia and other parts of the CIS. This makes trade and communication with other former Soviet countries easy

During winter, travelers to Estonia's islands often have an alternative to taking the ferry: the ice roads. The Estonian government evaluates the thickness of the ice to determine whether it is safe to open each of the country's seven official ice roads (which cover 50 miles/80 km of territory). Drivers must follow special rules to ensure safety when driving several miles over ice. Seatbelts aren't allowed, in case a quick exit from the car is needed. Cars must drive below 15 miles per hour (25 kilometers per hour) or between 25 and 43 miles per hour (40–70 kmh). Certain low speeds are unsafe, as they can create resonance waves that might break the ice. Perhaps due to these safety precautions, there have been no incidents of vehicles falling through the ice in Estonia.

and allows Estonia to act as a bridge between the other Baltic countries and Russia, as well as beyond into the Central Asian republics. The Via Baltika is a 600-mile (970 km) highway that connects Tallinn with the Polish capital of Warsaw. The highway then continues on to the Czech Republic capital of Prague, offering a continuous road from the Baltic coast into Central Europe. It is the most important road connection of the Baltic states.

If traveling by public transportation, most Estonians choose to go by bus, with daily buses from Tallinn to virtually every town and village in the country. In recent years, Estonia's passenger rail network has been cut back, with few regular services beyond the suburbs of Tallinn and less frequent long-distance services to Tartu, Pärnu, and Rakvere. There are daily international services to Saint Petersburg and Moscow.

A ferry crosses the Gulf of Finland.

International airlines such as Air Baltic, SAS, Finnair, Lufthansa, EasyJet, and Nordica provide direct flights to forty destinations from Tallinn.

Estonia's main ports—Tallinn, Pärnu, Kunda, and Sillamäe—are vital to the country's transportation system, providing a historic gateway from Western Europe that leads deep into Russia and beyond. A number of ferries, hydrofoils, and catamarans cross the Gulf of Finland to Helsinki each day, and there is a daily ferry service to the Swedish capital of Stockholm.

INTERNET LINKS

https://e-resident.gov.ee
Sign up to become an e-resident of Estonia at this government website.

https://www.lonelyplanet.com/estonia
This travel guide website provides information for visitors to Estonia.

https://www.visitestonia.com/en
This is the official website of the Estonian Tourist Board; it offers a wealth of information to potential visitors.

ENVIRONMENT

Estonia's coastal wetlands are known for their natural beauty and appeal to artists and tourists from Estonia and abroad.

5

DESPITE THE NATURAL BEAUTY AND rural character of much of Estonia's coastal regions, pollution and environmental degradation are major challenges for the nation. During the Soviet era, industrial development was often pursued without consideration of environmental consequences. When the Soviet Union collapsed and Soviet troops withdrew from Estonia, they left behind a lasting legacy of pollution. Rather than disposing properly of materials such as jet fuel and chemicals, they simply dumped these materials onto the land. The area around the Tapa Airfield was so contaminated that the water became undrinkable and residents developed health conditions in response to environmental pollution. However, most Estonians have access to clean, safe drinking water.

"When it comes to environmental issues, state borders must be crossed and it must be decided how we can help those countries that are directly influenced by the bad environmental condition. As is known, state borders mean nothing to the environment and the fact that the situation is bad in a particular place will sooner or later reach elsewhere."

—Estonian Minister of the Environment Siim Kiisler

The Soviet regime did have some positive environmental side effects, however. Inefficient farming methods caused an increase in woodland, providing habitats for local wildlife. In addition, many coastal areas were out-of-bounds for military reasons, and so many beautiful beaches and coastal reedbeds remained unspoiled for fifty years. The wetlands of Estonia's coasts and islands, as well as the peat bogs and forests of the mainland, were able to develop as sustainable environments for local wildlife. These areas now contribute significantly to Estonia's tourist economy.

More recently, Estonia's postindependence economic boom, especially the development of the oil-shale mining and timber industries, has also had a damaging impact on the environment. Estonia is one of Europe's largest air polluters. The oil-shale industry provides Estonia with energy independence but makes Estonia the world's leader in per-capita sulfur dioxide pollution. Toxic emissions decreased when the economy slowed during the 2008 global financial crisis, but as the economy recovered, emissions again accelerated.

The Estonian government is working to reduce pollution. In 2011, Estonia reached its goal of sourcing 25 percent of its power from renewable resources. This was achieved largely due to government subsidies of alternative energy. Additionally, the oil-shale industry, motivated by pollution taxes, has begun to reduce waste, but there is still room for improvement. A 2017 Organization for Economic Cooperation and Development (OECD) report concluded that Estonia "needs to move faster to reduce its dependence on oil shale so it can advance towards a greener economy and reduce air pollution and waste generation."

POLLUTION

Much of the pollution has been caused by Estonia's attempt to become self-sufficient for its energy. The county of Ida-Virumaa, in the northeast of Estonia, is heavily polluted as a consequence of the oil-shale mining and power plants that are crucial to meeting Estonia's energy needs. Oil shale is used to provide power to Estonian homes and industry and has allowed the country to become almost entirely self-sufficient in power generation since independence. Oil shale is extracted through surface mining, which in itself is a dirty process that damages the land and the local environment. The crushing and loading

of oil shale causes noise pollution and spreads dust, while the processing of oil shale uses up huge amounts of water.

More than 19.8 million tons (18 million metric tons) of oil shale are burned in thermal power plants at Narva each year, emitting 379,923 tons (344,660 metric tons) of sulphur dioxide. This gas not only pollutes the air in northeastern Estonia but is also carried by the wind across the Gulf of Finland, allowing it to pollute Finland's forests.

After oil shale has been mined, mining waste such as spent shale and ash has to be disposed of. The waste material usually takes up a larger area than the material extracted and so cannot easily be buried underground. It is calculated that in Estonia the mining of 1 billion tons (907 million metric tons) of oil shale creates approximately 360—370 million tons (327—336 million metric tons) of solid waste, of which 90 million tons (82 million metric tons) are mining waste, 70—80 million tons (64—73 million metric tons) are semicoke, and 200 million tons (181 million metric tons) are ash.

This power plant in Tallinn attempts to combat pollution by using ecologically friendly energy generation from secondary raw materials.

Estonia's natural resources include peat bogs. Peat, a soil-like material formed of decomposed vegetation found in marshy areas, can be harvested and used as fuel and fertilizer. During the Soviet occupation, many of Estonia's peat bogs were drained, making room for trees and other kinds of vegetation. Surprisingly, today these drained bogs are

one of Estonia's major sources of carbon emissions. As layers of vegetation decompose, they release carbon gases into the atmosphere. The solution to this problem is simple: restoring water sources to these drained bogs allows a living layer of moss to grow on top of the peat, thereby "capping" the bog and trapping carbon emissions within. Estonian environmental scientists hope to restore dried peat bogs to stop carbon leakage.

To avoid contaminating groundwater, toxic solid waste—such as heavy metals and sulfates—are disposed of in landfills. The oil-shale mines around Kohtla-Järve have created great slag heaps, and the landscape is dotted with hills made from the ash from the oil-shale power plants. Rain washes the toxic metals and organic compounds of these mountains of waste into the sea. As a result, the waters of this part of Estonia are so polluted, no swimming or fishing is allowed in the local lakes and rivers.

Estonia is committed to developing cleaner technology to save the ecology of the northeast region, although this is proving to be an expensive project.

WATER POLLUTION

In 2005, the United Nations International Maritime Organization named the Baltic Sea as a Particularly Sensitive Sea Area (PSSA)—one of only sixteen

PSSAs in the world—because of its high level of pollution. As a member of the EU, Estonia has been committed to cleaning up its waterways and upgrading its sewage system.

AIR POLLUTION

Oil shale—fired power plants cause air pollution, sending nitrogen oxides, sulfur dioxide, and hydrogen chloride, as well as ash, into the air. The mining of oil shale gives off more carbon dioxide emissions than does conventional oil production.

Estonia signed the 1997 Kyoto Protocol, which targets the reduction of greenhouse gases. The Estonian government has created legislation that punishes companies that do not handle industrial waste properly, but OECD experts say Estonia still has a long way to go. In 2016, the Estonian legislature (the Riigikogu) ratified the Paris Climate Agreement with fifty-five votes. In 2017, speaking at the United Nations Climate Change Conference, Siim Kissler, Estonia's minister for the environment, described the Paris Climate Agreement as a "promise to the world to protect the planet from climate change."

NATIONAL PARKS AND PRESERVES

Because its population is small and thinly spread, Estonia has many wetlands, forests, bogs, and coasts undisturbed by human activity. The Estonian government has made a firm attempt to protect the country's natural heritage.

KIHNU

Traditional social organization in some parts of Estonia still reflects the history of a people tied to natural rhythms and resources for their subsistence. On the tiny island of Kihnu, in the Baltic Sea, men go out to fish, sometimes for months at a time. As a result, Kihnu has been governed by women for centuries. Women continue to be in charge of all political and social decision-making on the small island. Men's contribution to society has been exclusively economic. This pattern continues into the twenty-first century, with women leading this community of six hundred.

ESTONIANS

Estonian teenagers dress in traditional clothing.

6

WHILE ESTONIA HAS A RELATIVELY small population (1.3 million people) it is an ethnically diverse nation. The diversity of its people reflects Estonia's history and geography. The majority of the nation is comprised of ethnic Estonians, descended from the migrants who came from Siberia thousands of years ago. Ethnic Estonians make up 69 percent of the population. Ethnic Russians, who make up 25 percent of the population, are the second-largest ethnic group. Their presence in Estonia reflects the nation's history as a member of the Soviet Union. The other major ethnic groups in Estonia are much smaller: Ukrainians (2 percent), Belarusians (1 percent), and Finns (1 percent). Other minorities include Tatars, Jews, Latvians, Poles, Lithuanians, and Germans.

"With an Estonian person, you never know if we're happy or sad. Or angry. Or excited. Most Estonians hide their emotions extremely well and throughout time it's been encouraged to hold it all in, as laughing and crying too excessively is a sign of bad manners. I believe this characteristic was a side effect of the not so expressive communist mindset, and thankfully the younger generations who are born in the free country are much more worldly and open."

—Kerli, from VisitEstonia.com

Many people left Estonia during the first years of independence. Polls carried out in 1989 and 2000 show that the population of Estonia decreased by at least 194,000 people, or about 12 percent, during those years. According to a 1989 census, the population was 1,565,000; by 1997, the number had fallen to 1,464,000; and in 2009, the population was estimated to be even lower, at 1,299,371.

This decrease is partly due to the halt in migration from the former Soviet Union, increased migration to Western European countries after Estonia joined the EU in 2004, and a drop in the birthrate. Estonia's population is declining.

Contemporary Estonian poet Kristiina Ehin writes about the complexities of articulating Estonian national identity while living in a linguistically mixed small country often overshadowed by other European nations. In her poem "How to Explain My Language to You," she writes:

I'm sitting with you
handsome Indo-European man
on a big mossy Finno-Ugric stone
the talk half-naked
night-bright between us

I so want to tell you
how pine trees smell in my language
and irises
how water babbles in my language over granite stones
and how crickets get the very last out of their fiddles

ESTONIAN PEOPLE

Estonians are a Finno-Ugric people, one among an ethnolinguistic group that includes the Finns, the Lapps, and the Hungarians. They first arrived in Estonia six thousand years ago, having journeyed across the Asian landmass from the marshes of Siberia.

Estonians are not related to their Baltic neighbors, the Latvians and the Lithuanians, who are Indo-European peoples. Ethnically and culturally, Estonians are close cousins to Finns and have more in common with them than with the other Baltic people. Estonians feel themselves to be very Scandinavian and not at all linked to Slavic people.

Estonians are traditionally a rural people. In Estonia today, the rural areas are dominated by ethnic Estonians, some of whom still pursue the traditional vocations of farming, forestry, and fishing. Ethnic Estonians are not evenly spread across the country. In thirteen of Estonia's fifteen counties, at least 80 percent of the people are of Estonian background. In fact, Estonians make up 98 percent of the population in Hiiumaa and Saaremaa. However, in the more urban Harjumaa, which includes the capital, Tallinn, ethnic Estonians make up just 60 percent of the population, while in Ida-Virumaa in the northeast they are a minority. Among the cities, Tartu is rare in being predominantly Estonian in ethnic makeup and character.

Estonians are a Finno-Ugric people. They share a linguistic family with the Finns, Lapps, and Hungarians.

CULTURE

Estonians are typical north Europeans in that they are individualistic and enjoy solitude. This explains the popularity of country homes: in summer most Estonians like to retreat to their country houses for as long as possible. The Baltic peoples are generally calm in character and not given to great displays of passion or affection. Some visitors find Estonians cool and reserved and say they have mastered the art of being polite without being friendly. The Slavic peoples, especially the Russians, tend to be more expansive and openly affectionate, offering hugs to each other when meeting. Estonians shy away from open displays of affection and tend to negatively associate such behavior with their least favorite neighbor. For Estonians, friendship is highly prized and not easily proffered.

A traditional
Estonian
country home

ESTONIAN ETHNIC AND NATIONAL IDENTITY

Although Estonians were, for much of their history, dominated by foreign powers, Estonians began to develop a national identity following the national revival of the late nineteenth century. For Estonians, ethnic identity is the essence of their nationhood. As a part of the Soviet Union, Estonians were not allowed to express their cultural separateness, except through officially recognized "Socialist realism" art forms, and were instead encouraged to adhere to the Communist Party ideal of the Soviet citizen—a "universal" human dedicated to international socialism. This ideology never appealed to the individualistic Estonians.

As a result of nationalistic feeling, Estonians have turned resolutely toward the West to find a new lifestyle and sense of purpose, one not dominated by Russia and communist ideology.

The town of Haapsalu is home to the Museum of Estonian Swedes, which displays traditional costumes and household textiles, as well as a tapestry telling the story of Estonia's Swedish community.

ATTIRE

As a result of their newfound affluence, Estonians dress very similarly to people elsewhere in the West. Long gone are the days of drab, Soviet-style suits. Western-made designer clothes can be bought in many shops in Tallinn. The long winters and cold weather mean that warm clothing is the norm; this includes heavy coats, sweaters, scarves, heavy boots, and thick socks.

Though there are regional variations, Estonians do have a recognizable national dress. Today it is often worn on festive occasions, especially for summer song festivals. Since independence, wearing traditional dress has become increasingly popular at national celebrations as a way of visibly expressing Estonian culture. Women wear long, heavy, woven skirts, gathered at the waist. The skirts are usually red, black, yellow, or orange and decorated with either fine vertical stripes or wide horizontal bands. If a skirt with vertical stripes is worn, it is usually combined with a heavy apron. A black or patterned belt holds the apron and skirt in place.

White, long-sleeved blouses are usually worn above the skirts, with wide, lace-edged collars and cuffs. The blouses are sometimes embroidered with floral designs and motifs. The collar is often fastened with a large, ornamental pin. Sleeveless bodices are also worn. The outfit is usually worn with white stockings and black shoes. Women often wear close-fitting caps or kerchiefs made of white linen and decorated with lace and silk ribbons. Journalist Andres Simonson notes, "The costume will require an ornate woven belt to finish the look and, more practically (because undergarments are strictly optional), to counteract gravity."

In Narva, over 90 percent of the population are Russian speakers, mostly Soviet-era immigrants or their descendants.

Estonian teenagers perform a dance in traditional dress.

This woman wears the traditional dress of the Old Believers, who fled to Estonia from Russia in the eighteenth century to escape persecution for their religious beliefs.

Estonian men wear black breeches, fastened at the knees with silver buttons, with a patterned vest over a white, long-sleeved shirt. The shirt is fastened at the neck with a braided tie or a pin. Sometimes a skullcap is worn on the head. Like the women, the men also wear white stockings and black shoes.

ETHNIC RUSSIANS

Russians make up roughly a quarter of the total population. Some Russians have lived in the Baltic countries since the eighteenth century, after Russia annexed the region from Sweden in the Great Northern War. In Estonia, most of these early migrants lived in villages around Lake Peipsi. Many of them were Old Believers, followers of a conservative form of Russian Orthodoxy who were persecuted in Russia proper. The vast majority of today's Russians in Estonia, however, moved to the country during the Soviet occupation. Some were encouraged to move as administrators in the Soviet government, while others moved to work in the industries of Estonia's northeast. Only about 40 percent of Estonia's Russian population were born in Estonia. Many retired Russian military personnel, especially officers, have chosen to remain in Estonia.

Today, Russians have a highly visible presence in the industrial towns of northern Estonia. In Narva, the vast majority of the people are ethnic Russians, and the populations of Kohtla-Järve and Sillamäe are primarily Russian as well. As a result, Ida-Virumaa has taken on a very Russian character. Even in the capital, Tallinn, half of the population is Russian. Sociological surveys reveal that most Russians identify themselves primarily with either Russia or their local city but not with the Estonian state.

The presence of a significant Russian minority has caused problems in Estonia in the years since independence. Russians without Estonian citizenship claim they are discriminated against in the workplace or treated as second-

STATELESS IN ESTONIA

Thousands of young ethnic Russians born in Estonia after the country's 1991 independence face the problem of statelessness. Citizenship laws changed in Estonia in 2016 to grant any children born in Estonia citizenship, but this does not impact young people born in Estonia prior to 2016. If their parents never became naturalized Estonian citizens, these young people are considered to be of "undefined citizenship, residing in Estonia," and the government issues them special gray "alien passports." They are not eligible to vote in Estonia, nor are they able to take advantage of EU membership by working abroad, as some young Estonians do. It can be difficult for these noncitizens to achieve Estonian citizenship, which requires fluency in Estonian. Many ethnic Russians who live in Russian-majority enclaves do not speak Estonian.

class citizens regarding salaries and public housing. Many perceived injustices are reported frequently in Russian mass media outlets, which are the main source of news for the Russian-speaking population, and they are a source of tension between Estonia and Russia.

Unfortunately, a linguistic barrier still exists and hinders full integration. For fifty years, Russian was the common language of the whole Soviet Union, and the Russians in Estonia did not need to learn to speak Estonian. Since independence, knowledge of Estonian is essential for education, business, and citizenship. However, with the growth of Russian nationalism in Russia, many ethnic Russians in Estonia have been reluctant to integrate, instead identifying more closely with their mother country. This has resulted in the alienation of ethnic Russians in Estonia.

OTHER ETHNIC MINORITIES

Before Soviet rule, many people from neighboring countries lived in Estonia, such as Swedes, Germans, Latvians, and Finns. These people had historical and cultural links with Estonia and were generally part of a small, educated elite.

Travel writer Rick Steves observes, "Strolling through the Russian market (in Tallinn), you feel tension. They are clearly the poor minority. And young Russian men can often make me uncomfortable. Their lives are tough. As I was passing a group of young Russians with heads nearly shaved bald, one of their phones rang. His ringtone was the sound of gunshots."

The Setos are a small group of Finno-Ugric people who inhabit the Setumaa region of southeastern Estonia and the formerly disputed Russian area around the city of Pechory, southeast of Estonia. The Setos have ancient ethnic and traditional ties with Estonians. In the Middle Ages, the Setos came under the control of the Russian principality of Pskov, and the region has been occupied by Russian troops for most of the time since. Over the centuries, the Setos drifted away from their Estonian counterparts and absorbed more Slavic culture and traditions, while Estonians were heavily influenced by German and Swedish culture. Most Setos are Russian Orthodox Christians and speak a dialect of the Võru tongue, common in southeastern Estonia.

Today's minorities are chiefly Slavic people who migrated from the former Soviet Union. Apart from Russians, there are significant numbers of Ukrainians and Belarusians in Estonia. Along with people from Azerbaijan, Armenia, Moldova, the Soviet Far East, and Siberia, these settlers were recruited by the government in Moscow to work in the construction, oil-shale, and power industries in the 1950s, 1960s, and 1970s. Separated from their homeland and discouraged from learning about Estonian culture, most non-Russians melted into the Russian-speaking population, learning Russian and sending their children to Russian-language schools. Consequently, in postindependence Estonia these people had difficulties assimilating with native Estonians.

The other major ethnic groups in Estonia are Jews, Latvians, Poles, Germans, and Lithuanians. The Latvians live mainly in the rural areas near the Latvian border.

In 1993, the Estonian government introduced the Law of Cultural Autonomy, giving all minorities the legal right to preserve and celebrate their identity, language, and culture. By 2007, more than two hundred ethnic societies promoting minority people had been registered—many funded by the government. Many are housed in the Estonian Nationalities Club in Tallinn, where cultural promotion and social activities are given priority. Orchestras have been developed, and handicraft groups and choirs have been formed. The Slavic Cultural and Charity Society revived traditional Russian song and dance festivals.

FINNO-UGRIC PEOPLE

Finno-Ugric peoples such as the Mordvinians, Karelians, Udmurts, and Maris also moved to Estonia as part of Soviet migration policies in the 1960s and 1970s. They came from areas west of the Ural Mountains and near the Volga River in Russia, and they are related to the Estonians by ancient linguistic and ethnic ties. Today, around three thousand non-Estonian Finno-Ugric people live in Estonia.

ESTONIAN SWEDES

Estonian Swedes have traditionally lived along the northwest coast of the country, around Haapsalu and on the islands. Before the Soviet occupation, as many as eight thousand Swedes lived in Estonia. Most fled the advancing Russian army in 1944. Now there are only a few hundred Swedes in the country.

INTERNET LINKS

http://www.erm.ee/en
This is the official website of the Estonian National Museum.

http://www.iisakumuuseum.ee
The Iisaku Museum provides a view of rural life in Estonia.

https://news.nationalgeographic.com/2016/10/setomaa-culture -estonia-russia-photographs
For photographs of Seto people and to hear the Seto anthem, see this *National Geographic* article.

LIFESTYLE

Tallinn features many bars and restaurants—including Olde Hansa, a medieval-themed restaurant.

7

DESPITE THE FACT THAT ESTONIAN national identity is derived from a sense of connection to the land, most Estonians (67 percent) live in urban areas, which increasingly resemble large urban centers in the West. Residents and visitors to Tallinn, for example, can patronize some the same chain shops and restaurants found in many nations of Europe. Distinctively Estonian forms of urban social life remain, however. In the winter, urban Estonians spend time in cozy cellar bars that shield them from the frigid temperatures.

Throughout Estonia, leisure and recreation hinge on the season. Estonians enjoy indoor activities during long, dark winters and seek to maximize every moment of the long daylight hours the northern nation enjoys each summer. Many Estonians travel to rural cottages in the summer or attend one of the country's many music festivals. Popular Estonian musician Kerli observes that Estonian culture is "the opposite of the American 'bigger, better, faster' mentality."

Estonians' ability to enjoy leisure and recreation opportunities today is a sharp contrast to the difficulties many Estonians endured when the

Higher education is free for Estonian students. As Prime Minister Jüri Ratas explains, "For our small and progressive country, the advantages of free higher education outweigh its disadvantages. For Estonia, it is crucial that our youth is educated, and their education corresponds to the needs of the labor market. We do not prepare our youth only for their first job, but also for life-long learning."

country gained independence from Russia. The transition from a Soviet, state-controlled economy to a free-market society was challenging. Many Estonians struggled with lack of food, fuel, and employment while the country transitioned to democracy and a Western-style free market economy.

URBAN LIFE

More than two-thirds of Estonians live in towns or cities. The center of Tallinn is still a pleasant place to live, with historic architecture, picturesque towers, and cobbled streets. The number of places to eat and drink in Tallinn has greatly increased since the Soviet era, when restaurants were few and service generally poor. Now most streets in the capital have a place to eat or drink. Cellar bars and cafés are very popular in urban areas, providing warm and cozy retreats from the winter weather. However, they are considered too hot and stuffy in summer, when Estonians prefer to be outdoors, in the countryside if possible. Nightclubs are also popular in Tallinn.

The goods in Estonian shops compare favorably with those available elsewhere in Europe and include chic fashions, especially in Tallinn. The

Tallinn's intact medieval Old Town became a UNESCO World Heritage site in 1997.

Scandinavian influence is apparent in the type of clothing found in stores in the capital. Western-style boutiques and barbershops are also increasingly common.

A new housing culture has developed in the past ten years, and many Estonians live in houses or newly built apartments of sophisticated, cutting-edge design. Estonia's newfound prosperity has led people to spend a lot of time and money improving their homes to make them more attractive and more comfortable.

Tenement blocks still ring many of Estonia's major cities, however, a leftover from the Soviet era. Tallinn's Old Town seems a world away from the drab housing developments of Õisemäe and Mustamäe south of the city. Many of Estonia's Russian minority live in these high-rise suburbs. A fifth of Estonians live in poverty, despite the country's growing economy, and overcrowding is a problem, with parents plus two children often squeezed into a one-bedroom apartment. Electricity and water supplies are often unreliable. There is still high unemployment in some urban areas, especially in Narva, Kohtla-Järve, and Sillamäe. The living standard in these cities is poor because of the horrendous pollution that characterizes the northeast of the country and causes health problems, especially lung and heart disease.

RURAL LIFE

About a third of Estonia's population live in the rural areas, almost all of them ethnic Estonians. Estonians feel themselves to be essentially country people. Following independence, many rural Estonians wished to return to the prewar idyll of the self-sufficient smallholder. The state-run collective farms were swiftly replaced by family-run farms that blossomed in the hands of their new owners.

Rural Estonians are far more traditional and less exposed to outside influences—not many speak a foreign language apart from Russian. Creature comforts are fewer in the country. People put in long, hard hours of manual labor and suffer the physical privations that come with long, cold, and dark winters. Some houses do not have running hot water or central heating, and wood is often stacked in neat piles around the house for fuel. Off the main highways, unpaved, dusty country roads lack proper markings or signs. Unlike

The Iisaku Museum, located in Johvi, Estonia, is housed in a building that used to be a ministry school. Now, it features exhibitions about Estonian rural life, farm tasks, and master craftsmen. In its collection you can find everything from thirteenth-century burial jewelry to modern rural crafts and traditional clothes.

in the cities, shops, businesses, and restaurants tend to close at 5 p.m., and everything is closed on Sundays. These inconveniences are offset by the advantages of breathing clean air, having plenty of space, and being able to indulge in picking wildflowers, berries, and mushrooms.

FAMILY STRUCTURES

The typical Estonian family is the small nuclear family, consisting of a mother, a father, and two children. It is rare for older relatives to live in the same house as their children and grandchildren. Estonians have developed a liberal, easygoing attitude toward marriage. More than half of the children are born out of wedlock. Estonia's birthrate has remained low for some years, with the average birthrate just 1.5 in 2016. In the Soviet era, the population increased mainly because of the arrival of immigrants from other parts of the Soviet Union. With immigration halted since independence, the population has been steadily declining. Child care and child rearing have become expensive in recent years, so couples prefer to raise a small family so that they can maintain their standard of living. In order to increase the birthrate, Estonia's government has instituted generous parental-leave policies so that both mothers and fathers may stay home with babies and young children.

An Estonian mother and her children enjoy time together in Tartu.

Although the marriage rate is low in Estonia, in recent years there has been an increase in the number of people marrying. More than half of couples live together before getting married, and many continue to cohabit without marrying. Divorce is increasingly common. This has led to quite a diversity of lifestyles in Estonia, with both the traditional extended family and the two-parent family being less common than in the past. Whereas in Latvia marriages between ethnic Latvians and minorities are common, in Estonia marriages between ethnic Estonians and Russians or other minorities are comparatively rare.

Traditional marriage practices have also become less common in Estonia. This is partly a result of fifty years of Soviet policies and partly because very few modern Estonians are religious.

LGBTQ RIGHTS

Estonia is considered to be the most lesbian, gay, bisexual, transgender, and queer (LGBTQ) friendly nation of the former USSR. Estonia decriminalized same-sex relationships in 1992. While gay marriage is not permitted, gay and lesbian couples have been able to register their relationship as a "cohabitation agreement" since January of 2016. While this gives them many of the same rights as married couples, gay and lesbian couples are unable to adopt children together.

SOCIAL CUSTOMS

Estonians are not known for their outward friendliness, and unlike Lithuanians and Latvians, they do not invite people they barely know to their homes. Estonians are not selfish or unfriendly, but they value friendship highly and do not offer invitations lightly.

Estonians browse a flower shop in Tallinn.

Estonians normally greet each other with a handshake, and some men may tip their hats. Bringing cut flowers when visiting is universal for any kind of gathering, celebration, or party, and they always prove a popular gift. Flower shops are found on nearly every street corner in towns and cities.

When Estonians entertain at home, it is usually to share a meal and drinks with family and close friends. Estonians are at their most relaxed when gathered around a table. Alcohol often features prominently. Drinking alcohol is a popular way of relaxing in Estonia, as it is throughout Scandinavia and the other Baltic states. Cheap alcohol is one of the primary reasons many Finns visit Tallinn for day or weekend trips.

AGING IN ESTONIA

Life expectancy is seventy-two years for Estonian men and eighty-two years for Estonian women. A high proportion of ethnic Estonians—one in five—are over sixty-five years old, and trends suggest that Estonia will support an increasingly elderly population. Before independence, young immigrants arrived from other parts of the Soviet Union. As a result, there is a greater proportion of young people among the ethnic minorities than among the rest of the population. The low fertility rates have also contributed to a disproportionately aging population.

In the past, not enough attention was paid to providing housing and services for the older generation. Now the government has had to invest in housing, social services, medical care, and transportation for this group. This need has placed severe demands on a developing and overstretched economy.

EDUCATION

Today, the aim of the education system is to promote Estonian language and culture and teach computer literacy and foreign languages. Most schools are run by the state, though private schools are slowly being introduced. According to the constitution, education is compulsory for all children from ages seven to seventeen. Higher education normally lasts for five or six years and is based on a credit system, in which students must gain a certain number of credits to complete their degree. Education in Estonia is based around the state curriculum, which is compulsory for all schools, whether state run or private.

The University of Tartu dates to 1632.

The University of Tartu, Estonia's oldest university, was established by King Gustavus Adolphus of Sweden in 1632. The language of instruction was Swedish, later to be replaced by first German and then Russian in the 1880s. Estonian was introduced as the language of instruction in 1919. It is estimated that one-fifth of the population of Tartu is either studying or working at the university.

Founded in 1938, the Estonian Academy of Sciences is Estonia's national academy of science.

At the University of Tartu, there is a famous sacrificial stone where students, having adapted a pagan custom, ritually burn their notebooks at midnight on the Thursday before their exams.

ELEMENTARY AND SECONDARY EDUCATION

It is compulsory for children to attend elementary and secondary school, beginning at age seven. Students are obliged to stay in school until they have completed their basic education or are seventeen. Most students graduate to

HIGH-QUALITY EDUCATION

Estonia is quickly gaining an international reputation for providing high-quality primary and secondary education. On international standardized tests, Estonian students ranked eleventh in the world, scoring higher than students in France and Germany. In Estonia, students begin to learn to program computers at the age of six, and digital literacy is taught alongside core subjects. Despite ethnic and socioeconomic diversity, Estonian schools manage to provide equal educational opportunities for all students, thereby shrinking the "achievement gap" between privileged and disadvantaged students common in many societies. The emphasis on providing equal educational opportunities is a holdover from the Soviet era. Marc Tucker, president of the National Center on Education and Economy in Washington, DC, visited Estonian schools and concluded: "What [we] saw in Estonia was not a new education system, it was an old one. By every account they did not change the system after the wall came down … It's hardly surprising they continued to get great results."

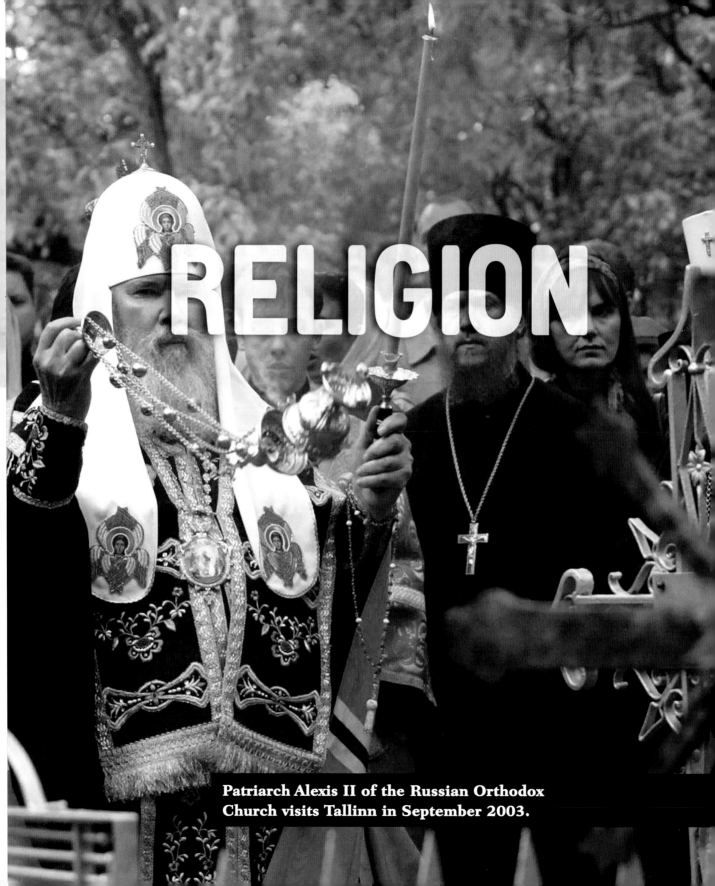

RELIGION

Patriarch Alexis II of the Russian Orthodox
Church visits Tallinn in September 2003.

ESTONIA'S HISTORY AS A COUNTRY frequently occupied by different ethnic and national groups has left it with a diverse legacy of religious institutions and beliefs, including Lutheranism, Catholicism, Orthodoxy, Judaism, and Islam. Today, most Estonians are secular in their outlook despite the fact that Lutheranism (a form of Protestantism) is the official state religion, and has been for five hundred years. "Estonia and the Czech Republic are the two nations that often claim to be the least religious in Europe. And they seem to be proud of their unbelief," Ringo Rigvee, a religious historian and advisor to the Estonian Ministry of the Interior, observes. Still, Estonia's constitution guarantees freedom of religion.

8

The current head of the Estonian Lutheran Church, Urmas Viilma, recently issued a call of welcome to Muslim immigrants arriving in Estonia. He encouraged the majority-secular Estonian public to talk about their Lutheran beliefs in order to better connect with Muslim newcomers, saying: "I'm quite confident that it's much more understandable for a Muslim if we speak about Christian values, instead of speaking generally and vaguely about European values."

ANCIENT RELIGION

Estonians' ancient cosmogony is still preserved in folkloric traditions. Before the forced conversion of Estonians to Christianity by the German crusaders, animistic beliefs held sway along the Baltic coast. Trees, rocks, hills, fields, and animals were worshipped as powerful spiritual forces. Much of this pagan religion was a product of the lifestyle of a hunter-fisher society at a time when trees covered most of Estonia.

Forests were thought to contain powerful spirits that could cause those who had behaved badly—especially those who damaged the forest—to lose their way or be attacked by forest animals. Springs, rivers, and lakes were also believed to contain spirits that could injure or kill the unwary. Spirits could be both protective and dangerous forces. The dead were also thought to inhabit the world as spirits and could be called on for assistance through funeral rites and sacrifices.

St. John's Lutheran Church stands in Tartu.

THE EVANGELICAL LUTHERAN CHURCH OF ESTONIA

Lutheranism—the dominant religion of most of Scandinavia and northern Germany—has been Estonia's official religion since it replaced Catholicism following the Reformation in 1520. Because of continuing warfare, however, the Lutheran Church developed slowly in Estonia, remaining a superficial influence until the establishment of a state church by Swedish rulers in the seventeenth century. Estonians were unable to gain direct access to the teachings of the church until an Estonian edition of the New Testament was published in 1686, making religion more accessible to the common people. In the early 1700s, the Moravian Brethren arrived in Estonia to begin a popular lay-Christian movement. The Brethren were suppressed by the Lutheran Church, but they left a lasting tradition of informal home schooling and literacy. A full translation of the Bible was written in 1739, and religion was taught in newly established schools.

Lutheran practices suffered during the czarist years because of the state's overt promotion of the Orthodox Church. But in 1919, the church was reorganized and renamed the Estonian Evangelical Lutheran Church, for the first time coming under Estonian control. In Estonia's first period of independence (1920—1940), the Lutheran Church flourished, and 80 percent of the population were officially listed as members. Following the Soviet occupation in 1945, religious worshippers were persecuted by the atheist communist state. It was not officially a crime to be a religious believer, but it was against the law to teach religion to children. Two-thirds of Estonia's clergy disappeared in the early years of Soviet rule, and many churches were confiscated or closed down. By the 1970s, fewer than 10 percent of Estonians, many of them Baptists, were prepared to publicly claim adherence to Christianity. In the late 1980s, as part of the liberating effect of glasnost, the religious repression lifted. There was a surge of interest in the Lutheran Church. The church allied itself to

Lutheran worship is characterized by its simple, austere style.

the burgeoning independence movement, and Estonians wanted to express their newfound freedom by celebrating everything Estonian. The number of baptisms rose tenfold, although this initial enthusiasm quickly waned. Today, there are approximately 165 Lutheran congregations in the country, with approximately 180,000 members. The Lutheran Church in Estonia began ordaining women pastors in 1967. As of 2018, 43 of Estonia's 212 Lutheran pastors are women.

Lutheran practice is far more austere than that of the Catholic and Orthodox faiths. The preaching of sermons plays an essential role in the service, as does the singing of hymns. Lutherans observe just two sacraments: baptism and the Lord's Supper, or Holy Communion. Church rites include confirmation, ordination, marriage, and burial. Confirmation is normally given between the ages of ten and fifteen and includes baptism and public profession of the faith by the recipient.

THE RUSSIAN ORTHODOX CHURCH

Members of the
ancient Russian
Orthodox sect the
Old Believers have
lived on the shores
of Lake Peipsi since
the eighteenth
century. The first
members came to
Estonia to avoid
persecution under
Czar Peter the
Great. They reject
traditional Orthodox
leadership and
conduct church
services in Old
Church Slavonic, a
medieval language.

The Russian Orthodox Church in Estonia was officially established in the eighteenth century following Estonia's absorption into czarist Russia. Promoted by the Russian bureaucracy, Orthodoxy had moderate success, due in part to the peasants' desire to find an alternative to Lutheranism, perceived to be the religion of the German landlords. In the nineteenth century, Orthodox membership rose as high as 20 percent. Czar Alexander III commissioned the construction of Orthodox churches throughout Estonia. The Alexander Nevsky Cathedral, built in the 1890s, is the most famous of these and stands on Toompea Hill in the center of Tallinn.

Since independence, the status of the Orthodox Church has been a source of friction between Russia and Estonia, as well as within the ethnic Russian and Estonian Orthodox congregations in Estonia. In the early 1990s, negotiations were held between the Constantinople and Moscow patriarchs over the status of Estonia's Orthodox communities, many of which wanted

Russian Orthodox churches are known for architectural ornamentation and the use of ritual in worship.

to return to Constantinople's jurisdiction. In 1996, the Constantinople patriarch decided to restore the Estonian Orthodox Church to its jurisdiction, much against the Moscow authorities' wishes. Orthodox Estonians were allowed to choose whether they wanted to continue with the Moscow-centered faith or become a part of the church under Constantinople's jurisdiction.

The Alexander Nevsky Cathedral in Tallinn is part of the Orthodox Church.

Today, the Estonian Orthodox Church, which has a mainly ethnic Russian congregation and is subordinate to the Moscow patriarchate, has thirty congregations with an estimated 170,000 members, while the Estonian Apostolic Orthodox Church, which is an autonomous church subordinate to Constantinople, has sixty-one congregations with roughly 25,000 members. The current leader of the Estonian Apostolic Orthodox Church is Stephanos, Metropolitan of Tallinn and all Estonia, elected in 1999.

Ritual is an important part of worship for the Russian Orthodox Church and includes music, the burning of incense, and chanting. Icons are positioned around the inside of most churches, and walls are covered with frescoes depicting religious events and symbolizing religious ideas. Believers pray in front of the icons, lighting candles as offerings and often kissing the icons as a sign of respect and supplication. The experience is intended to convey the mysterious essence of the faith. In contrast, the Estonian Orthodox Church is more austere in character, and its services and churches lack the colorful decoration and pageantry of their Russian counterparts.

OTHER CHRISTIAN SECTS

Other Christian religions, such as the Baptists, the Methodists, and the Seventh-Day Adventists, have been growing in popularity in Estonia. There are an estimated six thousand practicing Catholics in Estonia, many of whom come from Estonia's Polish, Ukrainian, and Lithuanian minorities. The Baptist and Methodist Churches have proved popular with some Estonians, who have sought new forms of Christian worship outside the Lutheran and Orthodox faiths. Jehovah's Witness and Mormon congregations also flourish.

RELIGIOUS DIVERSITY

Many non-Christian religions are practiced in Estonia today, chiefly by ethnic minorities who came to Estonia during the Soviet period. Additionally, the more mystical elements of traditional Estonian religion have contributed to the rising popularity of holistic beliefs such as the Hare Krishna movement. Neo-pagan religious movements have arisen in recent years, finding their roots in earlier forms of Estonian spiritual practice aimed at nature worship. In ancient times, Estonians would gather under oak trees before making important decisions. Estonia's most famous sacred tree, the Pühajärv Oak, long decorated the country's two-kroon banknote. Standing 65 feet (20 m) tall between a cow pasture and a lake, the Pühajärv Oak is believed to be the oldest and biggest oak in the country. In 1841, this famous tree became the site of unrest when peasants fought their German landlords over harsh and exploitative working conditions. In a BBC interview, Andres Heinapuu explains, "The tree doesn't have ears. I think the question out loud in front of the tree. And then I feel somehow the answer be sent back."

The Tallinn Synagogue is known as the "heart" of Judaism in Estonia.

JUDAISM Before World War II, about 4,000 Jews lived in Estonia. Many of them escaped to Russia before the Nazi occupation. During the occupation, the remaining 1,000 Jews were murdered, and the Nazi officials triumphantly declared Estonia to be Judenfrei (free of Jews). Since World War II, a small Jewish population has reestablished itself. There are approximately 2,500 Jews living in Estonia today, mainly in and around Tallinn, where there is a synagogue.

ISLAM Estonia has very few Muslims; for many years, Estonia's Muslims hailed from the former Soviet republics of the Caucasus region and Central Asia. Today, Estonia is home to a small but growing number of Muslim refugees from Syria and Afghanistan. Estonian leader Riina Kionka, chief foreign policy advisor to the president of the European Council, argues that Estonia should work hard to welcome refugees "given Estonia's history, with so many of its compatriots having been welcomed by other countries as refugees after the Second World War and during the Soviet occupation."

INTERNET LINKS

http://www.eelk.ee/en
Visit the official website of the Estonian Evangelical Lutheran Church to learn more about one of the country's main religions.

http://estonianworld.com/life/estonians-the-nation-of-neo-pagans
Estonian World is an online independent Estonian magazine headquartered in Tallinn. This article examines the rise of neo-paganism.

http://www.orthodox.ee/welcome.html
This is the official website of the Estonian Orthodox Church.

LANGUAGE

ULUPEOMUUSEUM
ng Festival Museum

PEETRI KIRIK
St Peter´s Church

PÜHA JÜRI KIRIK
St George´s Church

KREUTZWALD
ment to F. R. Kreutzwald

LINNAMUUSEUM
City Muse

WC

UTS
ment to O. Lu

RAHVA
an National

LODJAKODA
River Barge

INFOP

Street signs in Tallinn indicate Estonia's
multilingual history and culture.

9

ESTONIAN IS THE FIRST LANGUAGE of almost all ethnic Estonians, and it is the national language of Estonia as well. Ethnic minorities in Estonia speak a variety of languages, including Russian, Ukrainian, Belarusian, and Finnish. A few Estonians speak German, Latvian, Lithuanian, Polish, Swedish, or Tatar as their first language. National identity is often tied to language, which is perhaps why the choice of Estonian as a national language has been controversial in the multiethnic country.

All citizens are required to speak the national language to a minimal level, regardless of their mother tongue. Consequently, Estonian has been introduced as the primary means of instruction in schools, mainly with the long-term aim of integrating non-Estonians into society. However, the government passed a law that permits local government administrative procedures in districts with a non-Estonian majority to be conducted in a minority language. In practice, this means Russian is used in much of the northeast of the country, while Estonian is used almost everywhere else.

The Estonian government has a bureau dedicated to ensuring that Estonian is used in public contexts and to promote knowledge of Estonian around the world. Legal scholar Kirsten Shoraka observes, "Adherence to the Law of Language, including the use of Estonian in public signs, advertisements and place-names, is monitored by a National Language Inspectorate (that) conducts spot-checks and has imposed administrative charges for violations."

ESTONIAN LANGUAGE

The poet Lydia Koidula was one of the foremost poets of the national "awakening" of the nineteenth century.

Nearly one million Estonian residents speak Estonian as their native language, Unlike Swedish, Russian, and German, which are derived from ancient Indo-European languages, Estonian belongs to the Finno-Ugric family of languages. The Estonian language shares a history with Hungarian, Finnish, and the languages of the Sami (sometimes called Lapps) in northern Scandinavia, the Livs in Latvia, and the Mari, the Khanti, the Mansi, and the Mordvins in the Russian Federation. It is most closely related to Finnish, and Estonians and Finns have little trouble understanding each other. Estonian also reveals traces of German influence, although many German loan words were "Estonianized" with the arrival of Estonian independence in 1919.

Johannes Aavik (1880—1973) is credited with introducing some important linguistic innovations, including expanding the Estonian vocabulary to include a number of Finnish words that offer greater flexibility. Finnish "loan words" have easily been incorporated into the language. In recent years, many English words have also become common.

Early written Estonian was strongly Germanic in character. The first text to appear in the Estonian language was a translation of the Lutheran catechism in 1535. A New Testament in the southern Estonian dialect did not appear until 1686, and a northern version was not published until 1715. Using the northern dialect as a basis, Anton Thor Helle (1683—1743) united the two dialects and translated the Bible in 1739. Käsu Hans wrote the first known example of secular Estonian literature, a poem in which he lamented the destruction of Tartu in the Great Northern War, in 1708. The language developed more fully with the flowering of an Estonian literary movement in the nineteenth century, which included the first native Estonian poet, Kristjan Jaak Peterson. Friedrich Kreutzwald's epic compilation, *Kalevipoeg*, established an authentic Estonian literary tradition, of which the poet Lydia Koidula was one of the greatest examples. Koidula's legacy is of national importance; her biographer Madli Puvel writes that Koidula's "patriotic poems were set to music already during her lifetime ... These were the songs which stirred Estonians in their initial quest for national independence

PRONOUNCIATION GUIDE

Estonian is considered one of the most beautiful languages in the world, perhaps because of its numerous elongated vowels and few harsh consonants.

a..... ah *as in "father"*
b..... *voiceless, similar to the* p *in "copy"*
(c)
d..... *voiceless, similar to the* t *in "city"*
e..... a *as in "hay"*
(f)
g..... *voiceless, similar to the* ck *in "ticket"*
h..... h *as in "house"*
i...... ee *as in "feet"*
j...... y *as in "yes"*
k..... k *as in "kitchen"*
l...... l *as in "lily"*
m ... m *as in "mother"*
n .... n *as in "not"*
o..... o *as in "hope"*
p..... p *as in "pot"*
(q)
r ..... *the* r *is rolled*

s ..... *like the English* s *but voiceless and weaker*
š ..... sh *as in "shoe"—appears only in foreign words*
z..... s *as in "is"*
ž..... s *as in "pleasure"—used only in foreign words*
t ..... t *as in "tall"*
u .... oo *as in "boot"*
v..... v *as in "violet"*
(w)
õ..... ir *as in "girl"*
ä..... a *as in "cat"*
ö..... u *as in "fur" but with rounded lips*
ü .... oo *as in "boot"*
(x)
(y)

In Estonian, double vowels elongate the regular vowel sound. Estonian is also famous for its unusual contrast of three degrees of consonant and vowel length. For example, koli *(KO-li, "junk") is pronounced with a short* o *sound, while* kooli *(KOH-li, "of school") uses a longer* o, *and* kooli *(KOO-li, "to school") an extralong* o.

aa .. a *as in "father"*
ee ... eh *as in the interjection "eh?"*
ii .... ee *as in "feel"*
oo... eau *as in "bureau"*
uu .. oo *as in "food"*

ää... *same as* ä *but with a more open mouth*
öö... *same as* ö *but longer and higher*
õõ... *same as* õ *but longer*
üü.. *same as* ü *but longer and clearer*

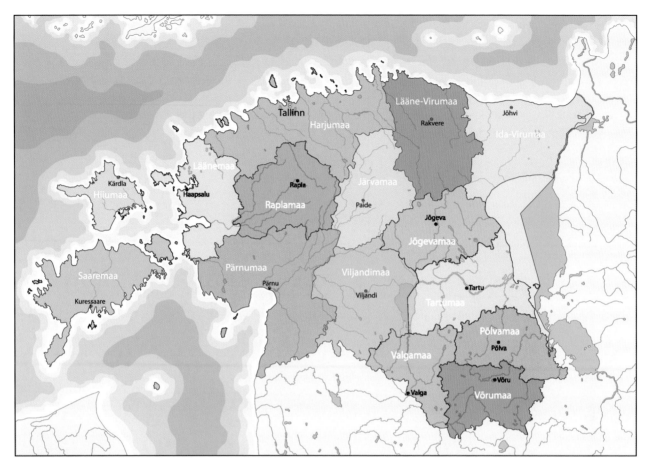

Labels on map: Tallinn, Harjumaa, Lääne-Virumaa, Rakvere, Jõhvi, Ida-Virumaa, Kärdla, Hiiumaa, Läänemaa, Haapsalu, Rapla, Raplamaa, Järvamaa, Paide, Jõgeva, Jõgevamaa, Pärnumaa, Pärnu, Viljandimaa, Viljandi, Tartu, Tartumaa, Saaremaa, Kuressaare, Põlvamaa, Põlva, Valgamaa, Võru, Valga, Võrumaa

This map shows the various counties, or *maakonnad*, of Estonia, in which different subdialects of the Estonian language are often spoken.

early [in the twentieth] century, and which, during the latter half formed a primary expression of Estonian national identity in the face of fifty years of Soviet occupation."

The Estonian alphabet is based on the Latin alphabet. It has twenty-three letters, plus nine foreign letters that have been borrowed for use from the many foreign words that have been adopted into Estonian over the years.

Estonian has a reputation for being a difficult language to master. The main challenge is vocabulary because Finno-Ugric languages have very few word roots in common with Indo-European languages. There are fourteen cases for each noun, while grammatical categories are usually marked by suffixes added to the stem of the noun or the verb. Verb endings, in contrast, follow very simple patterns, and there are no articles or genders. Similar to English, Estonian is an idiomatic language. For a country whose national identity is so closely associated with the land, it is not surprising to find Estonian surnames such as Meri (Sea), Kask (Birch tree), Ilves (Lynx), Maasikas (Strawberry), and Rohumaa (Grassland).

DIALECTS

Estonian has two major dialects: a Tallinn-based northern dialect and a more rural southern dialect. Recently linguists have divided Estonian into eight subdialects: northeastern coastal, central, insular (island), eastern, and western, plus three main dialects of the south: Mulgi, Tartu, and Võru.

ESTONIAN SWEDISH

Estonian Swedish belongs to the eastern group of dialects of the Swedish language. Isolated from the mother tongue, Estonian Swedish has many archaic characteristics and is not easily understood by modern Swedes. There are only about one hundred people in Estonia who can speak Estonian Swedish. Ordinary Swedish is popular for cultural and business reasons.

INTERNATIONAL LANGUAGES

English, German, and French are becoming increasingly popular. English and German are widely spoken in the tourist areas of Tallinn and Tartu. English is fast becoming a lingua franca among young people.

FINNISH Finnish is spoken in much of northern Estonia: it is estimated that at least five thousand people speak it as their mother tongue, while many more speak it as a second language. It is similar to Estonian. Many people of Tallinn, in particular, speak some Finnish because of the regular flow of Finnish tourists and businesspeople from Helsinki.

RUSSIAN Russian is a familiar language in Estonia. Until independence, many Estonians were required to speak Russian in order to communicate with the

Postimees, Estonia's oldest newspaper, has been published continuously for over 150 years.

authorities. Consequently, many Estonians are fluent in Russian, even if they rarely speak it.

PRINT MEDIA

Given its small population, the number and range of newspapers and magazines in Estonia is quite remarkable, with titles covering every conceivable subject. Seventy percent of all publications are published in Estonian. The main national Estonian-language newspapers include *Eesti Ekspress* (Estonian Express), *Eesti Päevaleht* (Estonian Daily), and *Postimees* (The Postman), which is Estonia's oldest newspaper and has been published in Tartu since 1857. *Postimees* and other newspapers also have Russian-language editions, but the most popular Russian-language daily is *Molodezh Estonii*. Estonian law guarantees freedom of the press, and local newspapers have been critical of the government. Foreign newspapers and magazines are also widely available. In addition, Estonia has a number of good-quality internet news services in Estonian, English, and Russian.

BROADCAST MEDIA

Television broadcasting improved greatly after independence, especially with the appearance of independent operators and foreign programming. There are several major independent television channels, as well as the state-run Eesti Televisioon (Estonian Television). The latter, which broadcasts programs in both Estonian and Russian, has a reputation for being dull and unimaginative. State-run broadcast media continue to receive government subsidies. Tallinn Commercial Television operates one channel that broadcasts in Estonian and Russian. Other commercial channels include Kanal 2, which broadcasts classic Estonian and Hollywood movies, and TV3, which offers American programming with Estonian subtitles. Cable television is widely available and offers programs in English, Russian, German, and Finnish.

While digital streaming services have globalized the media landscape, Estonians have limited access to the world's most popular streaming service, Netflix. In 2018, Estonian public broadcasting reported that only 15 percent of Netflix's catalog is available in Estonia. Due to the limited availability of streaming titles, broadcast and cable television enjoys larger audiences in Estonia than in other parts of Europe or in the United States.

For many years, people living in the north of the country have been able to watch Finnish television—in Tallinn as many as four Finnish stations are available. In the Soviet era, Finnish television offered Estonians a window on the Western world and a glimpse of another lifestyle. Finnish television remained popular until the Singing Revolution, when a surge of nationalism led to more pride in watching Estonian shows.

The Turkish foreign minister visits an Estonian morning show in 2008.

INTERNET LINKS

https://news.err.ee
This is the official web page of the publicly-owned Estonian broadcasting company.

https://news.postimees.ee/section/1476
This is the web page of Estonia's oldest newspaper, *Postimees*.

https://www.omniglot.com/language/phrases/estonian.php
Omniglot is an online dictionary of languages; this website features useful Estonian phrases.

ARTS

Contemporary Estonian art emerged from a national heritage that developed in response to occupying forces.

10

PRESERVING AND PRACTICING traditional arts and culture has been a challenge in Estonia due to centuries of occupation. Until the nineteenth century, Estonian culture was comprised largely of an oral tradition, poems and folktales shared over the generations. In the nineteenth century, during the country's national awakening, artists, writers and performers began to mine the country's legacy of folk material to promote a distinctively Estonian national culture which could be a bulwark against the norms and traditions of occupying forces. Contemporary Estonian arts evolved from this national heritage.

Perhaps the most visible and politically effective Estonian artistic movement of the twentieth century was Estonia's Singing Revolution (1987–1991). The Singing Revolution emerged from a popular environmental campaign that arose in response to the Soviet government's plan to mine phosphorite in Estonia—with potentially dire consequences for the land and people.

After pop stars began singing patriotic songs in tribute to Estonia—and in opposition to mining—singing traditional Estonian hymns and folk songs became part of a popular social movement. Crowds gathered to sing from a regular repertoire of songs, many of them dating from the nineteenth-century period of national awakening.

In June of 1988, the Old Town music festival was held in Tallinn. Spontaneously, the crowds began to sing these patriotic songs together. In 1989, two million people banded together and formed a human chain stretching throughout the Soviet-occupied Baltic states. Participants sang traditional songs in defiance of Soviet law and in protest of Soviet occupation. The Singing Revolution was a major factor in Estonian independence. When Soviet tanks sought to destroy Estonian radio and TV stations (and thus prevent the public declaration of Estonian independence), masses of protesters shielded the media stations with their bodies. Political scientist Stephen Zunes writes, "The Estonian revolution was led not by an elite vanguard of unsmiling ideologues. It was a massive, inclusive, and democratic celebration of a nation and its culture. Those values continue to resonate to this day ... They danced, and they had a revolution."

MUSIC

Music and singing are Estonia's most important and popular forms of artistic expression. The origins of folk singing in Estonia go back at least to the first millennium BCE as runic verse—short tunes with a limited range of notes but rich in variation. These songs were accompanied by traditional instruments, such as the *kannel* (KUHN-ehl), a kind of zither, along with whistles, pipes, flutes, and fiddles. Rhyming folk songs did not appear until the eighteenth century, when the Moravian Brethren congregations sang chorales in four-part harmony. The first Estonian arrangements of choir music were created in the mid-nineteenth century.

Estonia's first symphony orchestra was founded in 1900 in Tartu. Rudolf Tobias (1873—1918) wrote the first Estonian symphonic work, the overture *Julius Caesar*, in 1896 and followed this with Estonia's first piano concerto (1897) and oratorio (1909). Estonian symphonic music reached its peak in the country's first period of independence, between 1920 and 1940.

A large audience watches the Youth Song and Dance Festival in Tallinn in 2011.

The Estonian
Song Celebration
(Laulupidu) takes
place in Tallinn's
Song Celebration
Grounds every
five years in July.
The first festival
took place in Tartu
in 1869. Choirs
throughout the
country compete to
participate in the
festival, to combine
into a single choir;
in 2014, the most
recent festival,
thirty-three
thousand singers
participated. The
next festival will
be in 2019.

Estonia's first significant opera, *Vikerlased* (The Vikings), was written by Evald Aav (1900—1939). Eduard Tubin (1905—1982) wrote the first Estonian ballet, *Kratt* (The Goblin), in 1943. He fled to Sweden at the end of World War II to escape persecution under the Soviet occupation.

Veljo Tormis

Veljo Tormis (1930—2017) revived ancient forms of runic chanting and used them in his choral works. His best-known works, which are notoriously difficult to perform, are *Raua needmine* (Curse Upon Iron) and *Ingerimaa õhtud* (Ingrian Evenings), both part of a cycle of songs. The composer Alo Mattiisen (1961—1996) was known for using Estonian folk chants in some of his songs. Currently, Arvo Pärt (b. 1935) is Estonia's most widely acclaimed international composer, famous for his minimalist style and choral compositions. His best-known choral

The Tartu Music Festival, where the Singing Revolution got its start, was a small festival designed to nurture musical innovation. It was intended to support musicians as they freed themselves from censorship: both the censorship of the Soviet state, and the self-censorship required to succeed in a commercial market and appeal to popular tastes. The Singing Revolution arose from a festival that supported musical experimentation and innovation.

works are *Tabula Rasa*, *Saint John's Passion*, *Cantus in Memoriam Benjamin Britten*, and *Fratres*.

From October to April, classical performances are held almost every night at Tallinn's Estonian National Opera. In addition to housing the national opera company, it is home to the Estonian National Ballet and stages musicals and ballets. Tallinn is also home to the Estonian National Symphony Orchestra and the Estonian Philharmonic Chamber Orchestra and Choir. The choir has received fourteen Grammy nominations, including several for its recordings of works by Arvo Pärt. Small ensembles and solo performers also play in smaller halls and theaters in Tallinn, Tartu, and Pärnu.

Popular music, probably Estonia's most rapidly expanding art form, plays a major role in Estonia's celebrated summer music festivals. Both foreign and local rock, rhythm and blues, soul, and jazz bands have a wide following.

Few Estonian pop singers have succeeded internationally, although duo Tanel Padar and Dave Benton did win the Eurovision Song Contest in 2001. Rock music is still associated with the Singing Revolution of the late 1980s, a gesture of defiance that the Estonian people will remember proudly for generations.

LITERARY ARTS

Because Estonia experienced a long period of foreign domination, an Estonian-language literature developed quite late—in the middle of the nineteenth century, at the time of Estonia's national awakening. Kristjan Jaak Peterson (1801—1822) is considered Estonia's first original poet. Two writers remembered for their contributions to early Estonian literature—Friedrich Faehlmann (1798—1850) and Friedrich Kreutzwald (1803—1882)—were both doctors with a keen interest in Estonian folklore. Faehlmann collected verses of folk poetry from rural Estonia. After Faehlmann's untimely death, Kreutzwald continued his work. Between 1857 and 1861, Kreutzwald compiled and published Estonia's national epic, *Kalevipoeg* (Son of Kalev). The epic consists of 19,023 runic verses and tells the story of the mythical founder of the Estonian nation.

Postimees, Estonia's first Estonian-language newspaper, was founded in 1857 by Johann Jannsen (1819—1890). It contributed significantly to the national awakening. Jannsen's daughter, Lydia, who wrote under the pen name Lydia Koidula (1843—1886), produced some highly original and patriotic poetry. Many consider her collection of verse *Emajõe ööbik* (The Nightingale of Emajogi) to be the most important literary work from Estonia's period of national awakening.

Kristjan Jaak Peterson, nineteenth-century Estonian poet. His birthday is a national holiday called Mother Tongue Day.

Toward the end of the nineteenth century, writing novels became more popular. Eduard Bornhöhe (1862—1923) wrote romantic novels. His novel *Tasuja* (The Avenger), written in 1880, commemorated Estonia's troubled past by depicting the struggle against the German crusaders. The most prominent writer in the realism genre was Eduard Vilde (1865—1933). His novel *Külmale maale* (Banished), written in 1896, is a stylistic landmark in Estonian fiction. In the historical trilogy *Mäeküla piimamees* (Milkman of the Manor), written in 1916, Vilde portrayed the inequalities of the Baltic-German feudal system. He also wrote plays, including *The Unattained Miracle* (1912) and *The Fire Dragon* (1913). His contemporary Juhan Liiv (1864—1913) was a poet and storywriter whose most notable works are *Ten Stories* (1893), *Vari* (The Shadow, 1894), and *Poems* (1909).

A group calling itself Noor-Eesti (Young Estonia) sought to create a modern, cosmopolitan Estonian literature. Chief among them were Gustav Suits (1883—1956), Friedebert Tuglas (1886—1971), and Johannes Aavik (1880—1973). During the independence era, Siuru, a literary group that took its name from a mythical songbird, shocked conventional taste by exploring sensual and erotic themes. Marie Under (1883—1980) was by far the most gifted member of this

Voted the "Wonder of Estonia" by the public in 2012, the Tuhala Witch's Well is a naturally occurring geyser located in the village of Tuhala, where people have lived for about three thousand years. The Witch's Well provides a clear example of Estonian folklore connected to the local landscape. Located on terrain formed from limestone and other rocks that have been worn away, fissured, and

hollowed out by a network of underground rivers and springs, the Tuhala Witch's Well is one of many holes in the earth opening to water. When the river below floods, the well "erupts" with churning water. According to folk legend, the water erupts because witches in an underground sauna are beating one another with birch branches, thereby whisking up the water.

This still is from *Frank and Wendy*, Priit Pärn's cartoon series for adults.

century Russian plays. Well-known actors include Ita Ever, Tiia Kriisa, Andrus Vaarik, and Tõnu Kark.

FILM

From the beginning of the Soviet occupation until the political thaw following Stalin's death, Estonian filmmaking consisted of documentaries and newsreels, mostly of a crudely political style. Movies with artistic merit did not begin to appear until the 1960s. Kaljo Kiisk's *Hullumeelsus* (Lunacy, 1968) was the first, and it tackled social issues. Leida Laius's *Naerata ometi* (Smile Please, 1985) and *Varastadud kohtumine* (A Stolen Meeting, 1988) also received international recognition. Peeter Simm has directed historical movies, including *Ideealmaastik* (Ideal Landscape, 1980) and *Inimene, keda polnud* (The Man Who Never Was, 1989). More recently, Elmo Nüganen's *Nimed marmortahvlil* (Names in Marble, 2002) was praised for its realistic portrayal of Estonia's struggle against the Bolsheviks, while Ilmar Raag's

Klass (The Class, 2007) received critical recognition throughout Europe.

Above all else, Estonia has become famous for producing puppet and animated movies. Puppet moviemaking began in 1957 with Elbert Tuganov, who is perhaps best known for directing *Verine John* (Bloody John, 1974). Rein Raamat has achieved international success with his animated movies *Lend* (The Flight, 1973), *Suur Tõll* (Tõll the Great, 1980), and *Põrgu* (Hell, 1983). Priit Pärn has also received worldwide recognition for *Kolmnurk* (The Triangle, 1982), *Aeg maha* (Time Out, 1984), *Eine murul* (Breakfast on the Grass, 1987), and *Hotell E* (Hotel E, 1991), and for a television cartoon series for adults, *Frank and Wendy* (2005).

Today, experimental animators such as Mait Laas are gaining recognition for their surreal work, and cartoons such as *Leiutajateküla Lotte* (Lotte from Gadgetville) have gained critical acclaim at film festivals in Europe and beyond. In 2010, Kaspar Jancis's *Crocodile* was named Best European Animated Film at the Cartoon d'Or.

Sculptor Tauno Kangro's interpretation of Suur Tõll and his wife Piret. Suur Tõll (Tyll the Giant) is the mythical hero of the island of Saarema.

VISUAL ARTS

Estonia's first art school was opened at Tartu University in 1803, but Estonian national art did not really take off until the period of national awakening. In 1906, the first general exhibition of Estonian art was held in Tartu.

Following Estonia's first period of independence, Estonian art split into a plethora of schools, including cubism, abstract expressionism, and neo-impressionism. During World War II and the Soviet occupation, many Estonian artists fled to the West. In the 1960s, following Stalin's death, art again began to develop. By the 1970s, there were many artists and a thriving art scene in Estonia. Despite Soviet attempts to force Estonian art into the straitjacket of Socialist realism, Estonian artists maintained their connection with European traditions. One of Estonia's best-known artists, Erich Karl Hugo Adamson, commonly called Adamson-Eric (1902—1968), was famous for figurative painting and abstract design for ceramics and bookbinding.

Estonia's first feminist art exhibit, called Est.Fem, *was held in 1995. Reflecting on the exhibition, one of the curators, artist Mare Tralla (b. 1967), expresses disappointment in the outcomes of revolutionary artistic movements of the 1990s. She writes:*

Now Estonians are too involved in observing the glamour of capitalism and it is hard to believe in the idealism of the Singing Revolution ten years ago. All the society is oriented to male young and successful people. There are no forbidden ways to success—all progress is good. Even feminism as such is a good way as it may have some points of scandal in it and therefore be liked by the media. Some artists saw feminism merely as a fashion—a trend.

In her own work, Tralla explores gender tropes and ideals, feminism, and politics.

Other artists include surrealist Eduard Wiiralt (1898—1954), famed for his woodcuts, etchings, and book illustrations, and Kaljo Põllu (1934—2010), who was internationally recognized for his graphic art.

NATIONAL ARCHITECTURE

Estonia's architectural heritage is dominated by the Gothic style of the Germans and the Swedes, who ruled the country from the thirteenth to the eighteenth centuries and built many of its castles and fortifications.

Tallinn is one of the most architecturally diverse cities in the Baltic region and has some well-preserved medieval buildings in a predominantly German style. The city walls date from the fourteenth to the sixteenth centuries. Most of the guildhalls, churches, and residences in the Old Town and Toompea also date from this period. The best example of Renaissance architecture is the Blackhead's Fraternity Building in Tallinn, built in 1597, complete with intricately carved facade and portico.

The baroque style of architecture, dating from the seventeenth and eighteenth centuries, can be seen in Narva's restored Town Hall, originally built in 1671. Czarist Russian rule brought a more classical style of architecture to Estonia. Many of the manor houses that have survived in Estonia were built in this period, as were the main buildings of Tartu University and Tartu Town Hall. Nineteenth-century architecture was dominated by Baltic-German architects trained in Riga and Saint Petersburg.

By the 1920s, architects were trained for the first time in Tallinn itself. During this time the art nouveau style became popular, exemplified by the Parliament Building in Tallinn, completed in 1922. A more functional style dominated in the 1930s. Examples of this style are the Tallinn Art House and the Pärnu Beach Hotel.

In the Soviet period, emphasis was placed on cheap, practical, industrial housing. Many of these prefab monstrosities can be seen on the edges of towns and cities, especially in the northeast and around Tallinn.

The Town Hall in Narva

Estonia has some simple but impressive early churches, including the fourteenth-century Karja Church on Saaremaa Island and the ruined Jaani Church in Tartu. The Karja Church has many marvelous sculptures of medieval village life.

INTERNET LINKS

http://www.estonica.org/en/Culture
Estonia's online encyclopedia provides a wealth of articles on the history of the country's arts and culture.

http://www.kirmus.ee/est/info/in-english
This is the official Estonian Literary Museum website.

https://kunstimuuseum.ekm.ee/en
This is the official website of the Estonian Art Museum.

https://www.theguardian.com/music/tomserviceblog/2012/jun/18/arvo-part-contemporary-music-guide
The *Guardian* provides an overview of the music of Estonian composer Arvo Pärt.

LEISURE

A young girl forages for mushrooms in the forest.

11

ESTONIA'S NORTHERN CLIMATE shapes popular pastimes and leisure activities. Estonians take advantage of long, warm summer days by traveling to the countryside, the seashore, or visiting the nation's islands. Summer is also the season of music festivals, and choirs and musical groups are popular year-round pastimes across the country. One summer highlight is midsummer, the longest day of the year. Winters in Estonia are long, cold, and dark, but they provide ample opportunities for pursuing winter sports, such as skiing, ice-skating and tobogganing. Many wintertime leisure activities take place indoors, such as chess, a popular game in Estonia. In fact, the country's most famous chess player, Paul Keres, enjoyed international fame as a chess grandmaster.

During the Soviet occupation, luxury spas were run by the government, which encouraged working-class people to visit them. Government propaganda from the period reads: "Our working class heroes now enjoy relaxing vacations for the first time in their lives. All thanks to the government!"

OUTDOOR ACTIVITIES

In Estonia, attachment to the land is strong. Favorite summer pastimes are walking and picking berries and mushrooms in the woods and forests.

Camping on the coast, in the parks, or in the countryside is popular. Estonia has many campsites in the quiet rural areas. Estonia's lakes are sites for relaxation, and swimming is popular in summer. Some lakes, such as Pühajärv near Otepää, also have beaches. Pühajärv has a captivating, mystical atmosphere and was blessed by the Dalai Lama when he visited Tartu in 1992. Fishing is also a popular summer pursuit. In winter, people fish by cutting holes in the ice on the lakes.

Winter pastimes include ice-skating and tobogganing. Estonia's flat landscape and extensive winter snowfall make cross-country skiing a popular pursuit as well. The Otepää Plateau receives more snow than any other part of the country. The town of Otepää is Estonia's winter sports center—there is downhill skiing, ski jumping, and numerous cross-country routes for enthusiasts. Each February, about twelve thousand Estonians and foreigners brave the freezing weather to participate in the Tartu Ski Marathon, a cross-country skiing race.

TRAVEL AND RECREATION

Most urban Estonians take their summer vacation in the country, usually going to the national parks, islands, or picturesque regions in the south. The woods, islands, and lakes still offer a pristine freshness not found in many other parts of Europe. The low population density and undeveloped infrastructure mean buildings and fences rarely block a path or a view, giving the land an inviting openness. Pärnu is the most popular city destination.

Following the economic success since independence, more Estonians are taking vacations abroad. Finland and Sweden are by far the most popular foreign destinations, and they are quickly and easily reached by passenger ferry from Tallinn. Estonians also travel overland to Russia, Lithuania, Germany, and Latvia; some go as far afield as France, Spain, Italy, Britain, and the Netherlands. Flying long distance is still a luxury for Estonians, and few people travel as far as North America.

SPAS

Estonia is blessed with many health resorts, ranging from sanatoriums and spa towns to lakeside camps and curative mud baths. The sanatorium in Kuressaare on Saaremaa has specialized in baths of curative sea mud since 1876. The mud gives off a terrible smell, and only the most dedicated mud bathers endure the treatment.

Pärnu is famous for its promenade and beaches. The Baltic Sea's shallow waters make bathing both warm and safe in summer months. In winter, the water is ice-cold, and few people dare to swim.

Haapsalu is a popular resort town.

Haapsalu was developed as a spa town in the nineteenth century, though its curative mud is now considered of poor quality. A railroad was built to provide access to the town for the Russian aristocracy, and a long covered platform shelters visitors from the rain. Tchaikovsky, the famous Russian composer, often visited Haapsalu in summer, where he is said to have borrowed a motif from an Estonian folk song when composing his Sixth Symphony. The forested park and the beach of Paralepa near Haapsalu are popular with vacationers.

SPORTS AND ATHLETICS

Though Estonia is a small country, it has been successful in many international athletic competitions. Estonia participated in the 1920 Olympic Games shortly after gaining independence in 1919. Estonia continued to participate in the Olympics until the Soviet occupation in 1940. The 1980 Summer Olympics sailing regatta was held in Tallinn. After Estonia again gained independence in 1991, they participated in the 1992 Olympics in Barcelona, where Erika Salumäe

Kristina Šmigun-Vähi won an Olympic gold medal in cross-country skiing.

took the gold in cycling. Estonians have played a part in the Olympic Games ever since.

Traditionally, Estonians have excelled at wrestling. In 1901, Georg Lurich won the Greco-Roman wrestling world championship. Estonian wrestlers went on to win five gold medals at the Olympics before the Soviet occupation began. Estonian athletes also have an international reputation for track and field, weightlifting, judo, and sailing.

In the twenty-first century, Estonians have won four Olympic gold medals in cross-country skiing. Most recently, cross-country skiers Andrus Veerpalu and Kristina Šmigun-Vähi won gold medals in 2006 in Turin. The Estonian men's rowing team won the bronze in the 2016 Olympic Games in Rio de Janeiro.

Additionally, Estonia organizes and hosts international sports competitions. Recently, Estonia has hosted major athletic events such as the Biathlon European Championships and the World Junior Figure Skating Championships, both in 2015.

In addition to competitive athletics, sports are a popular hobby for Estonians. The Estonian Ministry of Culture reports that in 2014, 45 percent of Estonians practiced a sport for recreation. In the interest of public health, the Estonian government provides financial support for sports for children, adults, and professional athletes.

Basketball is the most popular sport in Estonia today. Its roots in the country go back to the 1930s, when neighboring countries Latvia and Lithuania won the European championships, and the sport grew in popularity during the Soviet period. Today, Estonia's basketball league features eight teams, including several from Tallinn, and the country fields teams in international competitions as well. Ice hockey and soccer are also popular sports.

SAILING

In a country with a long coastline and numerous islands, sailing is a natural pastime. The Baltic Sea is very shallow and freezes easily, so sailing is a summer

ESTONIAN ICE CRICKET

While the sport cricket is traditionally played on a field on warm summer days (of which Estonia has few), Coach Jason Barry of the Estonian national cricket team decided to reinvent the game on ice. An international tournament is now hosted every year. Traditional cricket players from the UK and elsewhere may find themselves sliding over the ice on frozen Lake Harku as they attempt to play the familiar game on a slippery surface.

activity. Estonia's waters are considered the best in the region for sailing, and the Pirita Olympic Sports Center is one of the best equipped. The center was built for the 1980 Olympic Games in Moscow, during which all the sailing events were held in Tallinn. Haapsalu is one of the few other places in Estonia to have a yacht club, which opened in 1992. It successfully hosted the World Ice Yachting Championship in 1991. There are many minor marinas in Estonia, and yachts, dinghies, and sailboats bob on the waters of fishing ports throughout the country.

INTERNET LINKS

http://www.estonianspas.eu/about/about-us
This is the Estonian Spa Association website.

https://www.spordimuuseum.ee
This web page belongs to the Estonian Sports Museum.

https://www.visitestonia.com/en/where-to-go/west-estonia /haapsalu
This Estonian Tourist Board page describes the spa town of Haapsalu.

FESTIVALS

Spectators watch a festive procession during the 1985 Estonian Song Celebration.

12

DURING THE SUMMER MONTHS, Estonians stage cultural events, especially in Tallinn, although smaller towns and cities host regional events. In small towns, residents may wear traditional clothing. Brewing and drinking beer are typical festival-day activities, and have been for hundreds of years.

Festivals, however, are not simply fun and games. Rather, they form part of the heart of cultural and political life in Estonia. In 1869, the country's first song festival celebrated Estonia's cultural and national awakening with music created in response to traditional folk stories and tunes. During the Soviet occupation, the song festivals continued even though it was ordinarily forbidden to publicly celebrate national identity. Music festivals helped Estonians hang on to their cultural heritage despite Soviet repression. In 1988, at the Baltica Folk Festival, the national flags of

Dancers perform at the 2014 Estonian Song Celebration.

"Today, as a member of the European Union, Estonia still clings to national song and dance as a pillar of identity. A recent study by the University of Tartu revealed that, in a country of 1.3 million people, nearly half have at one point participated in Laulupidu (the Estonian Song Celebration)."

—Rebecca Schmid, in the *New York Times*

Estonia, Latvia, and Lithuania were publicly displayed for the first time. That same summer marked the beginning of the Singing Revolution, where mass sing-along events served as public demands for independence. "For older people, [Estonian music festivals are] a national celebration of historical tradition," observes Estonian social scientist Marju Lauristin. "The younger the people, [the] more important is this togetherness—networking, being here with friends across Estonia and also the whole world."

MUSIC FESTIVALS AND EVENTS

Throughout the Baltic countries, song and dance festivals are held every summer. These events attract many visitors, especially Baltic people living abroad. The amphitheater of Tallinn's Song Celebration Grounds can hold up to 30,000 singers and has space for an audience of more than 150,000. Such is the popularity of singing festivals that there is rarely an empty seat.

The Estonian Song Celebration takes place every five years in July. This weekend event is the country's oldest song festival. In the most recent (2014) festival, a mass choir of 30,000 singers performed Estonian national songs.

Estonia hosts many other music festivals in the spring and summer months, including Jazzkaar, an internationally renowned jazz festival held every April in Tallinn; Muhu Future Music Festival, showcasing experimental popular, classical, and jazz music on the island of Muhu in early July; and the Blues Festival, held in August in Haapsalu.

PUBLIC HOLIDAYS

January 1 ....New Year's Day
February 24 ....Independence Day (1918)
March/April.....................Good Friday and Easter
May 1 ....May Day
June 23 ....Victory Day, marking the Battle of Võnnu (1919)
June 24 ....Saint John's Day/Midsummer Day
August 20..........................Day of Restoration of Independence (1991)
December 25 and 26 ....Christmas

CALENDAR OF FESTIVALS

April........... Jazzkaar: international jazz festival in Tallinn

May............ International Puppet Theater Festival: held in Viljandi's puppet theater

June............ Pühajärv Beach Party: pop festival with live bands and DJs

June 23....... Midsummer (Jaanipäev). The shortest night of the year features bonfires at hundreds of public and private celebrations

Late June.... Hansa Days: medieval-style fair with street performances and music in Tartu

July............. Beer Summer: gathering in Tallinn to taste local and international brews

July............. Viljandi Folk Music Festival: the most widely attended world music festival in the Baltic

August........ Days of the Seto Kingdom: folk festival in Obinitsa celebrating the culture of the Seto people

December... Dark Nights Film Festival: Tallinn's annual art-house festival

Smaller, local song festivals are held throughout the country. Since 1984, Estonia has hosted an International Organ Music Festival, usually held in early August, when some of the world's leading organists perform in Tallinn's beautiful, historic churches. The festival often moves around the country as well, playing in various locations.

FOLK FESTIVALS AND EVENTS

By far the most important folk festival in the Baltic is the Baltica Festival, held once every three years in one of the three Baltic countries each summer. The festival celebrates the folklore and culture of small, little-known ethnic groups throughout Europe. Folk dancers and singers from Estonia, Lithuania, and Latvia gather to celebrate the weeklong festival with dancing, singing, parades, and exhibitions.

There are numerous other folk festivals; for example, the Viljandi Folk Music Festival draws international fans and performers of world music. Every June, Tallinn Old Town Days celebrates traditional Estonian culture with much jollity, music, and dancing through the streets of the capital's Old Town. In May, Tallinn also hosts Lillepidu, an international flower festival that attracts thousands of spectators.

MIDSUMMER FESTIVAL

A Saint John's Day bonfire blazes.

The holidays of Võidupüha, or Victory Day, and Jaanipäev, or Saint John's Day, on June 23 and 24, combine the age-old pagan midsummer festival with the more modern, nationalistic celebration of the Battle of Võnnu, during which, in 1919, the Estonian army thwarted the Baltic German army's attempt to regain control of Estonia.

As can be expected from a region where summers are short and winters are long, dark, and cold, Midsummer Day—as Saint John's Day is also called—has been a major celebration since pagan times and is deeply rooted in Estonian peasant culture. Jaanipäev marks the longest day of the year, when the evening twilight and emerging dawn seem to become one. At this time of year, the light never fully fades. On the night of June 23 and the morning of June 24, villagers gather around a bonfire to sing, dance, and make merry.

In the past, the evening of Midsummer Day was considered a time of sorcery and magic. Purifying bonfires were lit to fend off evil spirits, and people would leap over them. Superstition had it that a successful clearance indicated a successful year ahead. Võidupüha and Jaanipäev usually merge into one long holiday.

INDEPENDENCE CELEBRATIONS

Estonians celebrate their independence.

Estonians celebrate their independence on February 24, the day the Republic of Estonia was first declared in 1918. The declaration was followed by a two-year war of independence, during which the fledgling Estonian army held off attacks by the Russian army and the Baltic German forces. The Tartu Peace Treaty of 1920 secured Estonia's borders for the first time in the country's history. Estonians take great pride in marking their hard-won independence, which serves as a permanent reminder of the Soviet Union's illegal fifty-year occupation. People celebrate by gathering to eat and drink, while the Estonian flag hangs from almost every building as an expression of national pride. The day is officially marked with the raising of the national flag at dawn from the tallest tower in Tallinn Old Town.

RELIGIOUS HOLIDAYS

The vast majority of ethnic Estonians are nominally Lutheran in faith. Although they celebrate the major festivals of Christmas and Easter, the Christian holidays do not create the kind of excitement or activity associated with the song festivals.

Christmas is celebrated in much the same way as in other northern European countries. On Christmas Eve, most Estonians celebrate by having a meal, visiting family and friends, and relaxing in their homes. Often the close proximity of the New Year provides them with an excuse to have a long midwinter break. Shrove Tuesday, during the seventh week before Easter, is usually observed in February. Children often go tobogganing on this day; it is believed that a long sleigh slide indicates a fruitful summer harvest. At Easter time, people dye eggs and give eggs as presents. Traditionally eggs were dyed using onion skins or leaves from birch switches. Shops, offices, and businesses are usually closed from the Thursday before Good Friday until the Tuesday after Easter Monday.

INTERNET LINKS

https://concert.ee/en
The main mission of Eesti Kontsert is to coordinate musical activity in Estonia, organize concerts, and initiate new music programs.

http://estonianworld.com/culture/estonian-song-celebration-timeline
Estonian World is a global independent online magazine, founded in London in 2012 and headquartered in Tallinn. This page features a timeline of the Estonian Song Celebration.

http://www.360pano.eu/dance_song_celebrations
This website offers virtual tours of Estonian song and dance celebrations.

https://tobreatheasone.com
This is the official website of *To Breathe as One*, a documentary on the Singing Revolution.

FOOD

A warm meal is served at a restaurant in Tallinn.

13

ESTONIAN CUISINE EMPHASIZES local, farm-fresh ingredients prepared simply and without spices. According to an Estonian proverb, "An empty belly is the best cook." Meat, starches, fruits, vegetables, and (when seasonal) berries, mushrooms, and nuts are staples of the diet. Dairy products, especially milk and cheese, are frequently used. Baking, roasting, and boiling are the most common ways of preparing foods.

Breakfast is a hearty meal, which might involve protein (in the form of salted fish, cottage cheese, ham, or hard-boiled eggs) as well as bread and porridge. Estonians drink coffee or tea with breakfast. Typically, lunch is served in three courses: a cold dish course followed by meat, potatoes, and vegetables with something sweet to follow, like a mousse, a sweet soup, or baked fruit. The evening meal is quite light, typically meat or pickled fish. Before eating, Estonians wish each other "Head isu!" (HEH-uht EE-soo), which roughly translates as "Enjoy your meal."

"There is one belief that is still followed in many homes—in case a piece of bread is dropped, it should be picked up and given a kiss in order to show a respect for the bread."
—from the Republic of Estonia Ministry of Rural Affairs

Rosolje, a beet and herring salad, is a lovely bright pink.

Food from the former Soviet republics in the Caucasus is very popular, especially šašlõkk kebab and grilled lamb.

GRAINS

Leib (LAY-p), or bread, is the essential staple of the Estonian diet and accompanies every meal. Because of food shortages in the past, bread has attained an almost religious significance among Estonians. Consequently, bread is never thrown away but often reappears in a different guise, such as in *leivasupp* (LAY-vuh-soop), a sweet, brown-colored bread soup.

Most Estonian bread is of the dark brown, wholemeal variety. Bread made from barley is a specialty and is often sweetened with honey. *Rukkileib* (RUK-kee-lay-p), rye bread enhanced with molasses, is also popular and a perfect accompaniment for Estonia's mild cheeses and spicy beer.

COLD DISHES

The first course in most Estonian meals is a selection of cold dishes. Traditionally, two-thirds of the meal consisted of cold dishes; as in Sweden and Russia, it is still considered the best way of showing off local produce. Often these cold dishes are as substantial as the main course. *Rosolje* (roh-SOHL-yuh), a delicious salad based on beets, meat, and herring, is the signature dish of Estonian cuisine. It is often served as a first course or a luncheon dish on a warm summer day. Small pies called *pirukas* (PI-ru-kuhs), filled with meat, carrots, and cabbage, are also served.

Fish—especially herring—is a part of the cold table. Estonia is famous throughout the region for its sprats (canned fish similar to sardines), which have been a local favorite since the Middle Ages.

MAIN DISHES

Estonian food is very much of the "meat and potatoes" variety, covered in a rich gravy. Potatoes were introduced in the eighteenth century and have been a mainstay of the Estonian diet ever since. Pork is the most important meat and is eaten in various forms: roasted, cured as bacon or ham, or in pies, sausage, and black pudding (also known as blood sausage). Sauerkraut (cabbage fermented in brine) is often served with pork.

SOUPS, DESSERTS, AND SOUP FOR DESSERT

Estonia's soups are generally bland, creamy dishes made chiefly from milk and vegetables, or perhaps with yogurt, dill, and cucumber. Unusually, many soups are eaten as desserts. *Kissell* (kee-SELL), a clear, sweet soup, is made from garden berries and red currants and served with white bread. Raspberry soup—liquidized raspberries boiled and whisked into a soup, then served with a dash of lemon and sour cream—is delicious, and many restaurants in Tallinn consider it their specialty.

"How, what, and where an Estonian eats seems largely to be determined by the length and warmth of the days. Darkness and frost bring sauerkraut and roast, brown and black pudding, thick soup and stew to the table. In summertime, on the other hand, people seem to survive on little but the warmth and sunlight, accompanied by everything light and fresh that gardens and forests have to offer."
—The Estonian Institute

Berries, apples, and rhubarbs appear in various guises—including stewed or baked in a pie. Baked apple is usually served with milk and sugar. *Mannapuder* (MAH-nah-pood-ah) is a kind of semolina milk pudding, similar to American cream of wheat, that can be found throughout Estonia. *Torten*, a favorite party dessert, came to Estonia as a legacy of the Baltic barons. Fluffy, plate-size pancakes, usually filled with raspberries or blueberries, are also popular. Sweet whipped cream is often added to cakes and pies.

BEVERAGES

Traditional drinks include ales and meads, teas brewed from plants found in the garden or the woods, and milk. Juices and cordials made from local summer fruit such as gooseberries, rhubarbs, and junipers have been enjoyed in the region for centuries. A preference for coffee over tea distinguishes the Baltic peoples from their Slavic neighbors, and coffeehouses and cafés are numerous throughout Estonia's cities and towns.

Lager and ale of the dark variety found in other parts of northern Europe have traditionally been brewed in Estonia. Saare beer, brewed on the island of Saaremaa, is considered one of Estonia's best traditional beers, while Saku Reval Luksus is a popular, Western-style, bottled beer. *Kali* (also called *kvass*) is a rye-based drink of Russian origin.

Popular spirits include cognac, vodka, and the locally produced Vana Tallinn liqueur. For many years, people in the Baltic countries have made their own moonshine vodka from rye.

RESTAURANTS

Since independence, the choice of both Estonian and international cuisines available in Estonia's towns and cities has dramatically improved. Tallinn in particular offers Chinese, Korean, Italian, Mexican, Middle Eastern, and Indian food, as well as many restaurants serving hearty, traditional Estonian cuisine. Local fast-food chains offering pizza, pasta, salads, and burgers can be found in every part of the country, as can the better-known international

burger chains. After work, Estonia's cafés are swamped by people seeking good coffee and tasty pastries. Tallinn's many dark, stuffy cellar bars are great on atmosphere but badly ventilated, chiefly as a result of the traditional insulation against the harsh winter.

Estonians enjoy meals on restaurant terraces when the weather is warm.

INTERNET LINKS

https://estinst.ee/wp-content/uploads/2017/03/581_Estonian-Cuisine_ENG_2015_veebi.pdf
This brochure takes an in-depth look at Estonian cuisine.

https://estoniancuisine.com
This website features many traditional Estonian recipes.

http://estonianfood.eu/en/kategooriad/eat-estonian
This website includes recipes and information about Estonian cuisine, including typical ingredients that are used.

https://www.visitestonia.com/en/why-estonia/top-10-unique-estonian-foods-to-try
This official government website lists ten Estonian foods everyone should try.

MUST LEIB (BLACK BREAD)

Makes 2—3 loaves.

½ cup (173 grams) unsulfured molasses
1½ cups (350 milliliters) warm water
1 (¼ ounce/7 g) envelope active dry yeast
1 tablespoon instant coffee granules
1 tablespoon unsweetened cocoa
1 tablespoon salt
1 teaspoon caraway seeds
2 cups (240 g) whole-wheat flour
2 cups (240 g) rye flour
1½ cups (180 g) unbleached all-purpose flour
¼ cup (113 g) coarse cornmeal
1 egg white, lightly beaten

Stir molasses into warm water, then add the yeast and stir until dissolved. Cover with a towel for 10 minutes until foamy, then stir in the coffee, cocoa, salt, and caraway seeds. In a mixing bowl, combine the whole-wheat, rye, and all-purpose flours. Add the wet ingredients, mix, and then place dough onto a floured surface. Knead by hand for 10 to 15 minutes. Gently shape the dough into a ball and put it into a greased bowl. Cover with a towel again and let it rise until it's more than doubled in volume, which should take about 3 hours. Knead the dough once more for several minutes and return it to the bowl. Cover and let it rise until doubled again, about 1 hour.

Cover a baking sheet in parchment paper and sprinkle cornmeal over it. Divide the dough into two equal loaves and place them on the baking sheet. Cover and let the loaves rise until doubled in size again, about 1½ hours. Then brush the dough with egg whites and cut two slits across the top of each loaf.

Preheat the oven to 400°F (204°C). Place a pan of water on the bottom rack and the baking sheet with the dough on the top rack. Bake for 35 to 40 minutes. Allow the bread to cool on the pan before removing.

LEIVASUPP (SWEET BREAD SOUP)

1 pound (0.5 kilograms) sliced pumpernickel
  bread, crusts removed
8 ounces (227 g) lingonberry sauce
½ cup (75 g) dark raisins
2 Macintosh apples, peeled, cored, and diced
1 cinnamon stick
½ cup (100 g) granulated sugar
2 whole cloves
½ cup (118 mL) heavy cream, whipped
Cheesecloth
Kitchen twine

Toast the bread and cut into 1- or 2-inch
(2.5 to 5 cm) cubes. Put the bread cubes
into a large pot with 7 cups (1.6 liters) of
warm water. Let the bread soak for at least
30 minutes and then beat it with a spoon.
Mix in the lingonberry sauce, raisins, apples,
and sugar. Wrap the cinnamon stick and
cloves in cheesecloth, tie with twine, and add it to the soup. Bring the soup to a boil, reduce
the heat, and simmer for 10 to 15 minutes. Serve cold in small dessert bowls with some
whipped cream on top.

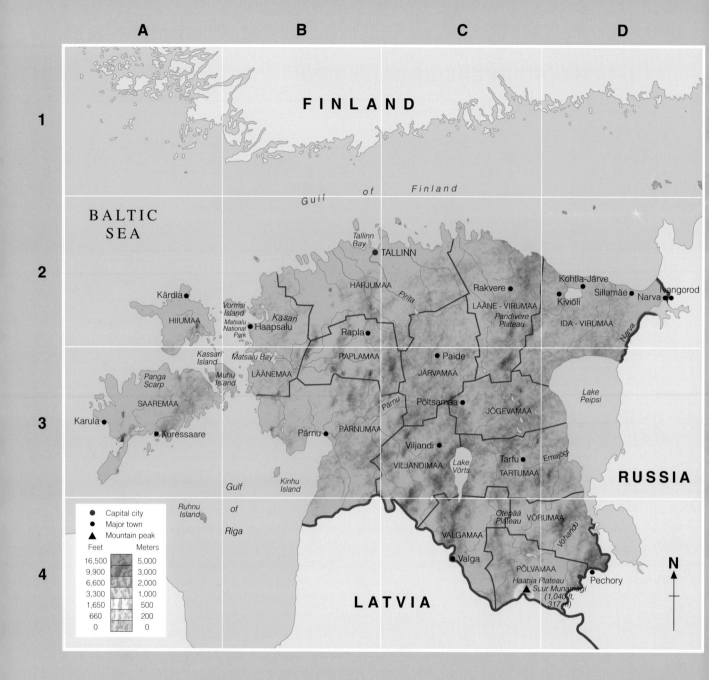

A   **B**   **C**   **D**

1

FINLAND

Gulf of Finland

**BALTIC
SEA**

2

Tallinn
Bay

● TALLINN

HARJUMAA

Pirita

Rakvere
●

Kohtla-Järve
●
Kiviõli ●   Sillamäe ●   Ivangorod
Narva ●

Kärdla ●

LÄÄNE - VIRUMAA

*Pandivere
Plateau*

*Vormsi
Island*

HIIUMAA

*Matsalu
National
Park*

Kasari

Haapsalu
●

Rapla
●

IDA - VIRUMAA

Narva

3

*Kassari
Island*

*Panga
Scarp*

SAAREMAA

Matsalu Bay

LÄÄNEMAA

*Muhu
Island*

RAPLAMAA

Paide
●

JÄRVAMAA

Põltsamaa
●

Pärnu

*Lake
Peipsi*

Karula ▲

Kuressaare
●

Pärnu ●

PÄRNUMAA

JÕGEVAMAA

Viljandi ●

VILJANDIMAA

*Lake
Võrts*

Tartu ●
TARTUMAA

Emajõgi

RUSSIA

*Kinhu
Island*

Gulf

*Ruhnu
Island*

of

Riga

Otepää
Plateau

VÕRUMAA

Vohandu

VALGAMAA

4

●	Capital city
●	Major town
▲	Mountain peak

Feet	Meters
16,500	5,000
9,900	3,000
6,600	2,000
3,300	1,000
1,650	500
660	200
0	0

Valga ●

PÕLVAMAA

Pechory ●

Haanja Plateau
▲ *Suur Munamägi
(1,040 ft,
317 m)*

LATVIA

N

MAP OF ESTONIA

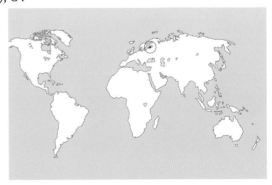

ECONOMIC ESTONIA

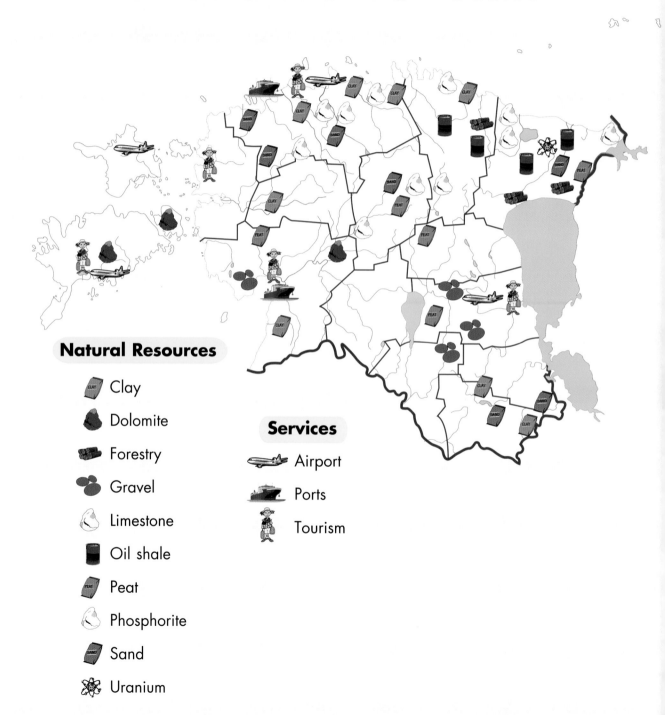

Natural Resources

- Clay
- Dolomite
- Forestry
- Gravel
- Limestone
- Oil shale
- Peat
- Phosphorite
- Sand
- Uranium

Services

- Airport
- Ports
- Tourism

ABOUT THE ECONOMY

OVERVIEW

Estonia has a modern market-based economy and one of the highest per-capita (per-person) income levels in Eastern Europe. Since independence, Estonia's various governments have put into practice free-market, probusiness policies and reforms. Estonia became a member of the EU in 2004 and adopted the euro as its currency in 2011. Estonia has strong trade ties with Finland, Sweden, and Germany, with the electronics and telecommunications industries a source of export and import business. Similar to those of many other countries, Estonia's economy slowed and fell into recession in mid-2008, but it has since recovered, with the economy growing 4 percent in 2017.

GROSS DOMESTIC PRODUCT (GDP)

$25.68 billion (2017 est.)

GDP PER CAPITA

$31,500 (2017 est.)

CURRENCY

Euro

LABOR FORCE

670,200 (2017 est.)

LABOR FORCE BY TYPE OF JOB

Agriculture: 3.1 percent
Industry: 20.2 percent
Services: 76.7 percent (2017)

UNEMPLOYMENT RATE

8.4 percent (2017)

NATURAL RESOURCES

Oil shale, peat, phosphorite, clay, limestone, sand, dolomite, arable land, sea mud

MAIN INDUSTRIES

Engineering, electronics, wood and wood products, textiles, information technology, telecommunications

MAIN EXPORTS

Machinery and electrical equipment, 30 percent; food products and beverages, 9 percent;, mineral fuels, 6 percent; wood and wood products, 14 percent; articles of base metals, 7 percent; furniture and bedding, 11 percent; vehicles and parts, 3 percent; chemicals, 4 percent (2016 est.)

MAIN IMPORTS

Machinery and electrical equipment, 28 percent; mineral fuels, 11 percent; food and food products, 10 percent; vehicles, 9 percent; chemical products, 8 percent; metals, 8 percent (2015 est.)

CULTURAL ESTONIA

Tallinn Old Town

Tallinn Old Town is listed as a UNESCO World Heritage site for its well-preserved medieval architecture—such as the Crusader-built Toompea Castle, the fifteenth-century House of the Great Guild, and Town Hall Square.

Kumu Art Museum, Tallinn

Opened in 2006, the Kumu Art Museum is the largest art museum in the Baltic region and one of the largest art museums in northern Europe. The architecturally impressive building is located on 9.9 acres (4 ha) in Tallinn, next to Kadriorg Park, and displays Estonian art from the eighteenth century to the present.

Lahemaa National Park

Situated on a long stretch of indented coastline to the east of Tallinn, the park is marked by four distinctive peninsulas protruding into the Gulf of Finland. Lahemaa has some of the most beautiful and varied landscapes in the country, with deserted beaches, reedbeds, and lush forests home to most species of wildlife native to Estonia.

Toompea Castle

Built in the thirteenth century at the top of a limestone outcrop that looms over Tallinn's Old Town, this Livonian Order fortress was the nerve center of Christian medieval Tallinn and includes the imposing Pikk Hermann (Tall Hermann), a 164-foot (50 m) tower dating from 1371.

Vilsandi National Park

Located off the western shore of Saaremaa Island, this national reserve's offshore islets and reedbeds are home to a multitude of migratory birds.

Pärnu

Pärnu is home to one of Esonia's most impressive, unspoiled sandy beaches, where beautiful sunsets can be seen from a recently constructed boardwalk along the seafront. The seaside town is also an internationally recognized health resort, with curative mud baths and other health therapies.

Tartu University

The main, architecturally impressive seveneenth-century structure of what many Estonians consider the national university includes four museums and a botanical garden. Dozens of other historic buildings spread around Tartu belong to the university as well.

Setumaa

Setumaa is home to Estonia's most distinctive minority. The Setos retain their own dialect and culture, with artistic traditions that have died out elsewhere.

Piusa Sand Caves

North of the town of Obinitsa, in the southeast corner of Estonia, the Piusa Sand Caves are a series of sandstone chambers excavated over many decades by the glassmaking industry. The caves have since become an important habitat for bats and were designated a protected nature reserve in 1999.

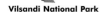

OFFICIAL NAME
Eesti Vabariik (Republic of Estonia)

TOTAL AREA
17,463 square miles (45,228 sq km)

CAPITAL
Tallinn

MAJOR CITIES
Tartu, Narva, Kohtla-Järve, Pärnu

COUNTIES (MAAKONNAD)
Harjumaa, Lääne-Virumaa, Ida-Virumaa,
Järvamaa, Jõgevamaa, Viljandimaa,
Tartumaa, Põlvamaa, Võrumaa, Valgamaa,
Pärnumaa, Läänemaa, Raplamaa,
Saaremaa, Hiiumaa

MAJOR RIVERS
Emajõgi, Pärnu, Narva

MAJOR LAKES
Peipsi, Võrtsjärv

HIGHEST POINT
Suur Munamägi (1,043 feet/318 m)

POPULATION
1.3 million (2017 est.)

LIFE EXPECTANCY
Total population: 76.9 years
Male: 72.1 years
Female: 81.9 years (2017 est.)

BIRTHRATE
1.6 children born per female (2017 est.)

ETHNIC GROUPS
Estonian, 68.7 percent; Russian,
24.8 percent; Ukrainian, 1.7 percent;
Belarusian, 1 percent; Finn, 0.6 percent;
other, 1.6 percent; unspecified, 1.6 percent
(2011 est.)

RELIGION
Lutheran, 9.9 percent; Orthodox,
16.2 percent; other Christian (including
Methodist, Seventh-Day Adventist,
Roman Catholic, Pentecostal), 2.2 percent;
other, 0.9 percent; none, 54.1 percent;
unspecified, 16.7 percent (2011 est.)

LANGUAGES
Estonian (official), 68.5 percent; Russian,
29.6 percent; Ukrainian, 0.6 percent;
other, 1.2 percent; unspecified, 0.1 percent
(2011 est.)

NATIONAL HOLIDAYS
Independence Day: February 24
Victory Day: June 23
Day of Restoration of Independence:
August 20

TIMELINE

IN ESTONIA	IN THE WORLD

800–1100 CE
Viking trade routes cross Estonia.

1206
Genghis Khan unifies the Mongols and starts conquest of the world. At its height, the Mongol Empire under Kublai Khan stretches from China to Persia and parts of Europe and Russia.

1219
The Danes conquer northern Estonia.

1227
German crusaders from Riga conquer and Christianize southern Estonia.

1346
The Danes sell northern Estonia to the German Livonian Order.

1535
The first Estonian-language book is published.

1558
Elizabeth I is crowned queen of England.

1561
Sweden conquers Estonia.

1632
Tartu University is founded.

1700
The Great Northern War, during which Russia conquers Estonia, begins.

1718–1736
Russian czar Peter the Great constructs the baroque, peach-and-white Kadriorg Palace.

1776
US Declaration of Independence is signed.

1789–1799
The French Revolution.

1816
Serfdom is abolished in Estonia.

1870
The Saint Petersburg–Tallinn railway is completed.

1914
World War I begins.

1918
Independence proclaimed after German occupation and the collapse of imperial Russia at the end of World War I.

1920
Peace treaty signed with Soviet Russia.

1934
Prime Minister Konstantin Päts leads bloodless coup and establishes authoritarian rule.

1939
World War II begins.

1940
Estonia is incorporated into the Soviet Union.

IN ESTONIA	IN THE WORLD

1941
Nazi Germany occupies Estonia.

1944
The German army retreats and Estonia is again occupied by the Soviet Union.

1945
The United States drops atomic bombs on Hiroshima and Nagasaki. World War II ends.

1988
Popular Front campaigns for democracy emerge amid the Singing Revolution.

1991
Communist rule collapses, and the Soviet government recognizes the independence of the Baltic republics.

1991
The Soviet Union collapses; occupied nations are granted self-governance.

1992
Lennart Meri becomes Estonia's first postindependence president.

1993
The European Union is created.

1997
Hong Kong is returned to China.

2001
Former Communist Party leader Arnold Rüütel is elected president.

2001
Terrorists crash planes into New York, Washington, DC, and Pennsylvania.

2003
In a referendum, Estonians vote overwhelmingly to join the EU.

2003
War in Iraq begins.

2004
Estonia is admitted to the North Atlantic Treaty Organization (NATO).

2008
Global financial crisis leads to worldwide recession.

2014
Estonia launches its innovative "e-residency" program.

2016
Kersti Kaljulaid becomes Estonia's first woman president

2016
The United Kingdom votes to exit the European Union.

2017
Estonia holds the presidency of the Council of the European Union.

2017
Donald Trump becomes the US president.

2018
Estonia marks its centennial anniversary.

2018
The Winter Olympics are held in Pyeongchang, South Korea.

GLOSSARY

Bolsheviks
Russian Communists.

glasnost
A policy of more social and political openness in the Soviet Union during the 1980s.

head isu (HEH-uht EE-soo)
The customary toast before commencing a meal.

Jaanipäev
Saint John's Day, as well as the celebration of the age-old pagan festival of Midsummer Day.

kannel (KUHN-ehl)
A musical instrument, like a zither, first used three thousand years ago, that has five to twelve iron or natural-fiber strings pulled taut over a board.

kissell (kee-SELL)
A clear, sweet soup made from garden berries and red currants.

leib (LAY-p)
Bread.

leivasupp (LAY-vuh-soop)
A sweet, black-bread soup, usually made from leftover bread, eaten as a dessert.

maakond (MAH-kont); plural, *maakonnad* (MAH-kon-ahd)
County; there are fifteen maakonnad in Estonia.

maarahvas (MAH-rahh-vuhs)
A term for Estonians.

mannapuder (MAH-nah-pood-ah)
A semolina milk pudding similar to cream of wheat.

perestroika
Russian word meaning "to restructure the political and economic system of a country"; a series of political reforms in the Soviet Union in the 1980s.

pirukas (PI-ru-kuhs)
Small pies filled with meat, carrots, and cabbage.

Riigikogu
The Estonian legislative assembly, or parliament.

rosolje (roh-SOHL-yuh)
Salad whose main ingredients are beetroot, meat, and herring; considered typically Estonian.

rukkileib (RUK-kee-lay-p)
Rye bread enhanced with molasses, the favored accompaniment for most Estonian meals.

torten
Rich German cakes.

Võidupüha
Victory Day, June 23, which is combined with Jaanipäev (see above) to make the midsummer holiday.

FOR FURTHER INFORMATION

BOOKS

Dragicevich, Peter, et al. *Estonia, Latvia, and Lithuania*. Oakland, CA: Lonely Planet Publications, 2016.

Hiisjarv, Piret, and Ene Hiiepuu. *Looking at Estonia*. Looking at Europe. Minneapolis: Oliver Press, 2006.

Jarvis, Howard, et al. *Estonia, Latvia, and Lithuania*. London, UK: DK Travel, 2017.

O'Connor, Kevin. *Culture and Customs of the Baltic States*. Culture and Customs of Europe. Westport, CT: Greenwood Press, 2006.

Taagepera, Rein. *Estonia: Return to Independence*. New York: Routledge, 2018.

Thomson, Clare. *Estonia—Culture Smart!: A Quick Guide to Customs and Etiquette.* London, UK: Kuperard, 2007.

FILMS

Ernits, Heiki, and Janno Põldma. *Lotte from Gadgetville*. Eesti Joonisfilm, 2006.

Tusty, James, and Maureen Castle Tusty. *The Singing Revolution*. Northern Lights, 2007.

MUSIC

Eller, Heino, et al. *Music from Estonia*. Scottish National Orchestra, conductor Neeme Järvi. Chandos, 2005.

Pärt, Arvo. *Te Deum/Silouans Song/Magnificat/Berliner Messe*. ECM Records, 1993.

Tormis, Veljo, et al. *Vision of Estonia* I. Alba, 2003.

BIBLIOGRAPHY

BOOKS

Clemens, Walter. *The Baltic Transformed.* Lanham, MD: Rowman & Littlefield, 2001.

Daitz, Mimi. *Ancient Song Recovered.* Hillsdale, NY: Pendragon Press, 2004.

Karner, Karin Annus. *Estonian Tastes and Traditions.* Hippocrene Cookbook Library. New York: Hippocrene Books, 2006.

Lauristin, Marju, and Peeter Vihalemm. *Estonia's Transition to the EU.* Evanston, IL: Routledge 2010.

Lieven, Anatol. *The Baltic Revolution: Estonia, Latvia, Lithuania, and the Path to Independence.* 4th ed. New Haven, CT: Yale University Press, 1994.

Page, Edita, ed. *The Baltic Quintet: Poetry from Estonia, Finland, Latvia, Lithuania, and Sweden.* Hamilton, ON, Canada: Wolsak and Wynn Publishers, 2008.

Raun, Toivo. *Estonia and the Estonians.* Stanford, CA: Hoover Institution Press, 2001.

Smith, David J. *Estonia: Independence and European Integration.* London, UK: Routledge, 2002.

Williams, Nicola. *Estonia, Latvia, and Lithuania.* 4th ed. Oakland, CA: Lonely Planet, 2006.

WEBSITES

Baltic Times. http://www.baltictimes.com.

Estonica: Encyclopedia About Esotnia. http://www.estonica.org/en.

The State Portal. https://www.eesti.ee/eng.

Statistics Estonia. https://www.stat.ee/?lang=en.

Tallinn Tourism. https://www.visittallinn.ee/eng.

US Department of State—Estonia. https://www.state.gov/p/eur/ci/en.

Visit Estonia. https://www.visitestonia.com.

INDEX

INDEX